The Adventures
of
Moccasin Joe

Photograph courtesy of Jack Strohm and Grace Howard Porter.

George S. Howard
1850–1887

The Adventures
of
Moccasin Joe

The True Life Story of Sgt. George S. Howard

CIVIL WAR DRUMMER BOY; TRAIN WRECK SURVIVOR;
WESTERN SCOUT, HUNTER, AND FISHERMAN; AND MURDER VICTIM—
WHO RECORDED HIS IMPRESSIONS IN PROSE AND POETRY.
HIS RECOLLECTIONS OF MONTANA, WYOMING, NEBRASKA, AND THE
DAKOTAS BRING THE WILD WEST TO LIFE.

Susan C. Reneau

Foreword by Jerome A. Greene

1994
Blue Mountain Publishing, Inc.
Missoula, Montana

The Adventures of Moccasin Joe

The True Life Story of Sgt. George S. Howard—Civil War drummer
boy; train wreck survivor; Western scout, hunter, and fisherman; and
murder victim—who recorded his impressions in prose and poetry.
His recollections of Montana, Wyoming, Nebraska, and the Dakotas
bring the Wild West to life.

Published in 1994

Library of Congress Card Number: 91-073719
ISBN Number: 0-9611376-1-4

Published in the United States of America by
Blue Mountain Publishing, Inc.
5425 Skyway Drive
Missoula, Montana 59801

(406) 251-5116

This book was printed on recycled paper using soy-based ink.

DEDICATION

To the people who love America and

individuals who have made this country great.

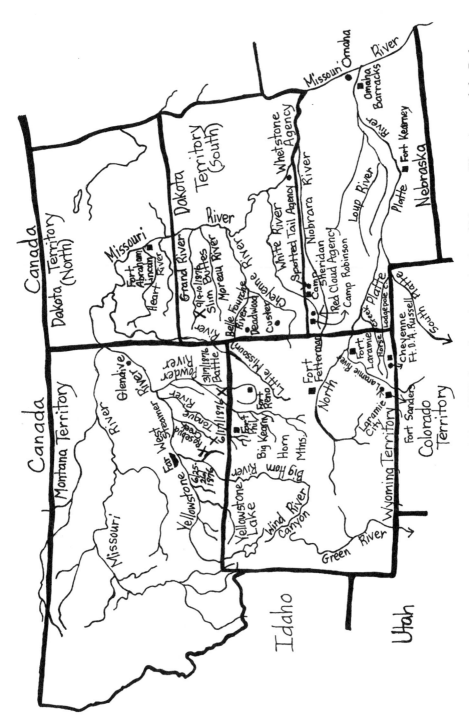

Map showing the travels of Moccasin Joe from 1872 to 1877 throughout the territories of Montana, Wyoming, and the Dakotas, and the state of Nebraska.

FOREWORD

The Adventures of Moccasin Joe represents a labor of love on the part of Susan Reneau, as is indicated by the years she has spent gathering supportive documentation and information to augment Moccasin Joe's (George S. Howard's) diary.

Her work embodies an important firsthand data source for one of the epic periods in American military history, that encompassing the great Sioux War of 1876–77—America's largest Indian war, and the nation's most important military undertaking since the end of the Civil War in 1865.

The conflict was famous for the battles of Powder River, the Rosebud, the Little Big Horn (including "Custer's Last Stand"), and Slim Buttes. George S. Howard was present at all of those engagements except Little Big Horn, and his diary contributes to the historical context of the wide spectrum of army operations during the conflict.

Although he had served with the volunteers during the Civil War (as a drummer boy), Howard's enlistment in the Second Cavalry Regiment of the Regular Army of the United States in 1872 was propitious for two reasons. First, from his vantage, it sustained the young man through the economic uncertainty that faced the country during much of the postwar period. Second, and ultimately most important, Howard's record of his military experiences during his five-year term included his involvement in the Great Sioux War.

While Howard's diary offers insights into general army life at western posts during the early part of his service, its major contribution clearly lies in Howard's description of events connected with the Sioux War from the standpoint of an enlisted participant. Whereas officer recollections abound, those penned by common soldiers are most decidedly rare. Thus, Howard's diary adds significantly to our knowledge of those events.

I first learned of Howard's diary when I was researching my own book, *Slim Buttes, 1876: An Episode of the Great Sioux War* (University of Oklahoma Press, 1982), and I encountered a published excerpt in *Winners of the West*, the tabloid of the long-defunct National Indian War Veterans Association.

But the entire diary, which included not only the full extent of Howard's entries, but his revealing poetry written both in garrison and in the field during the course of his service, eluded me until I learned of the present work.

Happily, the availability of Howard's effort, coupled with informed documentary perspective provided by Susan Reneau, affords a lasting contribution to our knowledge of the old army during the days of Crook, Custer, and Crazy Horse—the colorful, yet tragic, days of the Great Sioux War.

Jerome A. Greene
Arvada, Colorado

INTRODUCTION

Seldom in the lifetime of one American, does a person have the opportunity to work with an original piece of literature from more than 120 years ago. When the daughter of the diary writer entrusted me with this precious document, I felt obligated to do it justice. So began my quest to uncover the mystery of the pages of this handwritten diary of George S. Howard.

Many qualified individuals have helped me in my quest, but I feel several people need to be thanked at the start of this book.

Frederick H. Campbell, an attorney in Colorado Springs, Colorado, and a historian who teaches various early American and constitutional law courses at the University of Colorado and Colorado College, first encouraged me to research the contents of the diary. Throughout the process, he has been a guiding force who suggested contacts, libraries, and other historians. His advice and guidance cannot be underestimated.

Jack Strohm, my friend and uncle, introduced me to the diary writer's daughter, Grace Howard Porter, in 1976 when the country was celebrating its bicentennial. For two delightful years before she passed away in 1979, I talked to and wrote to Grace about her father and the diary. Without Jack I would never have met Grace. His love of American history and ongoing enjoyment of reading has been a great influence in my life.

Jerome A. Greene was first introduced to me when I read, and practically memorized, his book, *Slim Buttes, 1876: An Episode of the Great Sioux War*, in 1982. I began to research Howard's diary in 1977 shortly after receiving the original diary, and found several references to Slim Buttes in Howard's writings. Greene's book provided details about this battle that clarified Howard's words. Over the years, I have found Greene's research at the National Park Service to be critical in my understanding of the time period in which George S. Howard lived. I was deeply appreciative when Mr. Greene offered to read the book's manuscript and contribute the foreword.

Starting in 1979, I wrote to John J. Slonaker, chief of the historical reference branch of the United States Military History Institute at Carlisle Barracks, Pennsylvania. His reading list of books and magazines helped me understand the writings of George S. Howard. Mr. Slonaker spent countless hours reviewing the book's manuscript and making thoughtful comments about its organization and style.

INTRODUCTION

James S. Hutchins, an armed forces historian at the Smithsonian Institution's National Museum of American History also provided a valuable reading list in the 1970s and reviewed the book's manuscript in 1994. His time and energy to review the manuscript improved the final product.

Charles E. Hanson, Jr., director of the Museum Association of the American Frontier, also reviewed the book's manuscript and offered welcome comments to me throughout the final editing stage. Back in 1977, I wrote to him and received a list of important books to read related to the time period in which George S. Howard lived.

A cumulative thank you goes to all the staff at the National Archives in Washington, D.C., who over a 14-year period continually helped me locate original documents that related to the diary. Many of the staff took a personal interest in the preservation of the diary and spent many hours showing me how to properly encapsulate it to protect it from dust, dirt, and skin oils.

The artists who have graced the pages of the book with their sketches include Lori A. Scoffield of Pocatello, Idaho, Marv Enez of Powell, Wyoming, and Harold I. Hopkinson of Byron, Wyoming. Lori's original pen and ink sketches introduce Chapters One through Six and illustrate various aspects of George S. Howard's action-filled, but short, life. Harold's thoughtful portrayal of an Indian woman introduces Chapter Seven. A variety of thumbnail sketches depicting various aspects of Western life were done by Marv.

No word of thanks is complete without recognition of my husband, Jack, who assisted me with the ongoing and time-consuming research necessary to bring this original piece of 19th century literature to life. Jack, as an author and editor of fourteen books, and a wildlife biologist by trade, has the ability to tirelessly review documents and scan microfilm until he is satisfied he has the correct information. His personal involvement with this 14-year project was deeply appreciated.

A final word of thanks goes to Grace Howard Porter, daughter of the diary writer, who faithfully saved the diary from destruction and provided insight into her father's life through her charming letters and telephone conversations with Jack Strohm and me.

George S. Howard's gentle soul comes through powerfully in his writings. And, I hope the readers of this book will enjoy his life and times as much as I have in creating this story of a sensitive 19th century man. He is one of many sensitive men I love.

Susan C. Reneau

CONTENTS

MAPS AND ILLUSTRATIONS

The Adventures
of
Moccasin Joe

SCOFFIELD

Chapter One

Who Was This Moccasin Joe?

October 14, 1872, dawned cool and crisp for George S. (Shepard) Howard as he reached the steps of the recruitment office in Springfield, Massachusetts. For the first twenty-two years and six months of his life, George had enjoyed a rural existence as a New England carpenter and railroad worker. Much of his life had been spent studying the classics and reading the Bible, skipping rocks along the Connecticut River, and hunting for squirrels on golden autumn days.

George had been trained by his father to be a carpenter in the family construction business in Hinsdale, New Hampshire. He was born at home on April 9, 1850, as the sixth son of Cyrus and Louisa Phinney Howard and one of fourteen children. His formal education ended early in life, but his mother Louisa taught him from the Bible and encouraged her children to read a variety of classic literature. His daughter recalled he often spoke with great fondness about his mother and seldom mentioned his father, who died in 1878, shortly after George returned from his Western enlistment. When George was but 11-years-old in 1861, he took the birthday of his older brother, James, age 19, and enlisted in the Civil War on May 22, 1861. He became a drummer boy listed as a private in Capt. Draper's F Company of the 36th Massachusetts and marched into battle with adults.

The records at the National Archives include George S. Howard mixed with James' records, which made finding the muster rolls of George even more difficult. Reviewing muster rolls for all New England states took the better part of five years to complete, but what an interesting mystery was uncovered for my patience. The mystery was solved in the summer of 1991 when I pieced together the two men's records by reviewing the muster rolls of all Union soldiers in five New England states.

George served three years and spent the entire year of 1863 in Finley Hospital in Virginia suffering from an unknown illness. No one from his family filed for his pension, so few records of him in the Civil War remain except the muster rolls in the National Archives. He returned home at the age of 15 to work in his father's business.

Young boys often enlisted during the Civil War thinking the activity romantic. An enlistment also brought a meager monthly wage which was often sent home to a poor family. George lived in New Hampshire, but enlisted in Massachusetts to avoid detection. Hinsdale is a short horseback ride to the Massachusetts border, so it is assumed George thought it safer to travel that distance to mask his age.

This Vermont and Massachusetts Railroad passenger train crashed through Long Bridge near Athol, Massachusetts, on June 16, 1870, making the headlines of numerous eastern newspapers. The accident was announced in the New York Times on June 17, 1870, with the headlines, "Shocking Railroad Accident". The article incorrectly stated George S. Howard suffered a ". . .fatal fracture of the skull".

Recruitment of healthy soldiers in 1861 had reached a fever-pitch, so few birth certificates or other legal documents were ever checked when a young man told the recruiter his age. Few legal documents were available to the average person, except a family Bible, so recruits often just held up their hand and swore to tell the truth, the whole truth, so help me God. When a boy plans to go on an adventure, thoughts of lying about his age were not a great concern.

The average height of a man in the 1800s was under six feet, and George was probably tall for his age, so telling people he was an adult might have been easier for him. No written records of how his mother felt exist, but one can only assume she remained worried until his arrival home. As a mother of three sons, one of whom was 11 years old in 1993, I can't imagine the agony I would have felt if my son trudged off to the war with his squirrel rifle tucked under his arm.

Historians and staff at the National Archives said that if a commander of a unit discovered a young boy, he would often send him to a hospital for "treatment" until proper discharge papers could be gathered for the child's release to insure a safe haven for the young recruit. The early stages of the Civil War were romantic adventures for young boys who were tempted to try their wings and earn a little extra money at the same time.

George remained on the muster rolls until August 31, 1864, when he received a medical discharge from Assistant Surgeons William A. Bradley and John V. D. Middleton of Finley Hospital who received a note from the medical director's office in Washington, D.C., asking them to file a report on the physical condition of George. The note, dated December 11, 1863, read:

> "Sir: You will please examine Geo. S. Howard, 36th Mass. Vol., a patient in the Hospital under your charge, and if he is a fit subject for discharge, you will forward certificates of disability and report your action tomorrow morning, the 12th.
>
> Very Respectfully
> Your Obedient Servant
> (Can't read signature of doctor)
> Signed for the Medical Director"

The medical report was not in George's records, but a statement honorably discharging him did exist, so it is assumed the two surgeons gave a favorable report that allowed young George to go home to New Hampshire.

His brother James left for war as a private in Company E of the 8th Vermont Volunteer Infantry on February 8, 1862. He died of wounds suffered during a battle outside Port Hudson, Georgia, on June 24, 1863. His wounds, according to a War Department report dated November 7, 1889, included shots to the right side and arm. He was sent to a hospital in Baton Rouge, Louisiana, on June 13, and died there eleven days later.

George's father was chronically ill, according to the pension papers filed by Louisa on behalf of James in 1889. The small pension Louisa received from the death of James helped to support the family when Cyrus could not work as a carpenter and business owner. Financial hardship was a way of life for the Howard family, according to a medical report filed by the Howard family physician, Dr. H. Peirce, on behalf of Louisa's pension claim.

Records filed on behalf of Louisa show that James sent home $7 per month. After James died, the family received $60 on April 4, 1864, and Louisa received a pension of $12 per month until her death on July 28, 1893. George's service was never recorded completely, and no one from his family ever tried to apply for a pension.

George never mentioned his Civil War enlistment to his recruiting officer in 1872 for fear that he would be in contempt of the law. His daughter said he told her tales of his secret enlistment long after he returned from the West.

What occurred in 1870 at the age of 20 would profoundly influence George for the rest of his life. He had become a brakeman on the Vermont and Massachusetts Railroad in 1868, and, on June 16, 1870, as he worked aboard a passenger train that left Boston's station at 7:30 a.m., his train crashed headlong through a bridge railing into a river.

The front-page headline stories of the accident in the *Boston Daily Journal, New York Times, Boston Journal, Boston Morning Journal, Boston Post,* and the *Fitchburg Sentinel* give details of the tragedy. Copies of the newspaper accounts were found in the Library of Congress in Washington, D.C., and the Fitchburg Library in Fitchburg, Massachusetts.

The exact article, as it appeared in newspapers of the day, reads as follows:

"A terrible railroad accident occurred between this place (Athol, Massachusetts) and Royalston this morning (June 16, 1870), about 11 o'clock by which three persons were killed outright and twenty more frightfully mangled and bruised, some of the number past all hope of recovery.

"While Conductor Holden's passenger train, which left Boston at 7:30 o'clock, was on the point of rounding a curve near what is known as the Long Bridge, the engineer saw a hand-car standing on the bridge. He immediately reversed his engine, and did everything that man could to prevent the impending disaster; but the time was too brief after the discovery of the obstruction to arrest the speed of the train. The force of the collision caused the bridge to bend, and in a moment the engine was thrown from the track and tore with crushing force through the bridge into the river, dragging the baggage and one passenger car after it.

"The forward passenger car was thrown under the baggage car and the second passenger car piled on top of the baggage car. P. B. Morse, sectionmaster, was in charge of the hand-car at the time of the accident, and says that he made a mistake in looking at his watch and admits that he was where he ought not to have been at the time of the catastrophe. The engine, baggage car and one passenger car are completely demolished, and it is considered as miraculous that all the passengers in the forward car were not killed outright or badly injured.

"All the surgeons in Fitchburg arrived at the wreck soon after the accident, and the surgeons and citizens of Athol and Orange were promptly on the spot and rendered all the aid that was possible. Those injured are well cared for. Conductor Holden and all passengers not injured were prompt in rescuing the killed and wounded from the wreck, carrying them in their arms out of the river to Conductor Bangs' train, which was on the spot at once, and conveyed them to Athol."

THE UNITED STATES OF AMERICA.

OATH OF ENLISTMENT AND ALLEGIANCE.

State of *Massachusetts*
Town of *Springfield* ss. :

I, *George S. Howard*, born in *Hinsdale*, in the State of *New Hampshire*, and by occupation a *Carpenter* DO HEREBY ACKNOWLEDGE to have voluntarily enlisted this *Fourteenth* day of *October*, 1872, as a SOLDIER in the ARMY OF THE UNITED STATES OF AMERICA, for the period of FIVE YEARS, unless sooner discharged by proper authority: And do also agree to accept from the United States such bounty, pay, rations, and clothing as are or may be established by law. And I do solemnly swear, that I am *Twenty Two* years and *Six* months of age, and know of no impediment to my serving honestly and faithfully as a Soldier for five years under this enlistment contract with the United States. And I, *George S. Howard* do also solemnly swear, that I will bear true faith and allegiance to the UNITED STATES OF AMERICA, and that I will serve them honestly and faithfully against all their enemies or opposers whomsoever; and that I will observe and obey the orders of the President of the United States, and the orders of the officers appointed over me, according to the Rules and Articles of War.

George S. Howard (SEAL)

Subscribed and duly sworn to before me, this *14th* day of *October*, A. D. 187*2*.

F. Trent
Capt 4th U.S. Cavalry
Recruiting Officer.

I CERTIFY, ON HONOR, that I have carefully examined the above-named recruit, agreeably to the General Regulations of the Army, and that, in my opinion, he is free from all bodily defects and mental infirmity which would, in any way, disqualify him from performing the duties of a soldier.

F. Trent
Capt 4th U.S. Cavalry
Examining Officer.

I CERTIFY, ON HONOR, that I have minutely inspected the above-named recruit, *George S. Howard* previously to his enlistment, and that he was entirely sober when enlisted; that, to the best of my judgment and belief, he is of lawful age; and that I have accepted and enlisted him into the service of the United States under this contract of enlistment as duly qualified to perform the duties of an able-bodied soldier, and, in doing so, have strictly observed the Regulations which govern the Recruiting Service. This soldier has *gray* eyes, *dark brown* hair, *fair* complexion, is *Six* feet *two* inches high.

F. Trent (SEAL)
Capt 4th U.S. Cavalry
Recruiting Officer, United States Army.

[A. G. O. No. 73.]

Photograph courtesy of National Archives.

George S. Howard enlisted in Springfield, Massachusetts, on October 14, 1872, and headed for Fort Laramie, Wyoming Territory. This is his original enlistment paper in the National Archives, Washington, D.C.

Photograph by Jack Reneau.

Cyrus Howard built this house at the corner of River Road and Howard Street in Hinsdale, New Hampshire, for his family shortly after he purchased the land from Alexander Elmore in 1851. The front porch was added at a later date. The house is presently occupied.

Photograph courtesy of Grace Howard Porter.

*Cyrus Howard,
George S. Howard's father.*

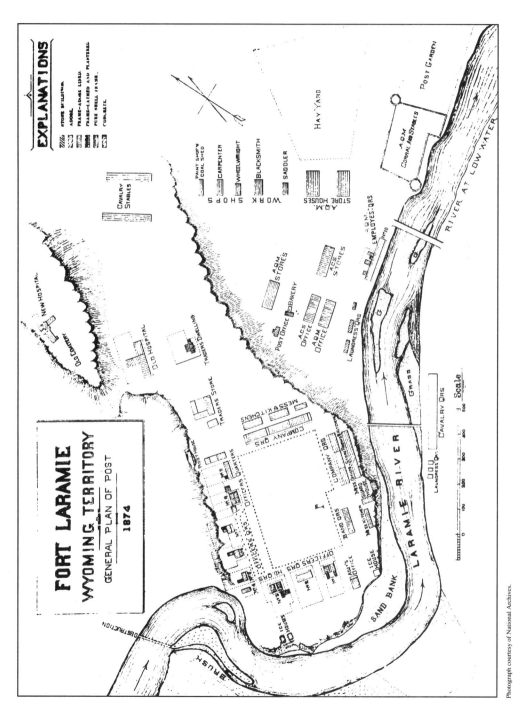

Photograph courtesy of National Archives.

This map shows the general plan of Fort Laramie in 1874 when George S. Howard was stationed there. The cavalry barracks are shown across the Laramie River.

This accident at Athol was listed as one of the three most serious train wrecks in 1870 by books found in the Association of American Railroads' research library.

Newspaper accounts in the *New York Times* listed George as fatally injured with a skull fracture and not expected to live. His daughter, Grace, recalled stories of the accident told by her father years later. She said that he had at first been left for dead as doctors and survivors searched for the treatable injured. As rescue workers uncovered twisted metal and wood from the crushed rail cars, George's fingers began to wiggle. Someone noticed the movement and dragged him from a twisted passenger car. An operation was performed on his fractured skull and a silver plate was inserted.

In actuality, the method of treatment was called trephining. The medical instrument, a trephine, lifted the fractured skull fragments from his brain. He may have received chloroform or chloroform mixed with alcohol as a primitive anesthetic, but medical journals of that time indicated few patients had such relief from the agony and danger of the operation. Grace recalls her father saying the procedure was very painful, indicating that little anesthetic was used. The *Boston Medical and Surgical Journal* of October 31, 1901, said that the method of trephining was not only antiquated but dangerous and not recommended unless all other treatments had been used. Often patients died of a cerebral hemorrhage, not from the skull fracture, but from the procedure. For George, the procedure was his only hope of survival.

George suffered greatly from headaches after the accident, and amnesia, disorientation, and erratic behavior later in life. When George began scouting for the Army at Fort Laramie, Wyoming, the Indians feared him and called him Scar Head the Crazy Scout because of the dramatic scar across his forehead.

He wrote that no man bothered him because they respected his scar. For this reason, George was able to travel alone or with one friend throughout the wilds of the Wyoming, Montana, Nebraska, and Dakota Territories without being attacked by various Indian tribes and hunted side-by-side with Indians without being harmed. His emotional mood swings, though, contributed to his premature death, less than ten years after leaving the Western frontier.

Journey to Fort Laramie

Amazingly, less than two years after the train accident in Athol, George recovered enough from his massive skull fracture to consider employment. Although guaranteed a job with the railroad for the rest of his life, George decided to enlist in the 2nd Cavalry, Company E, as a scout and private. He served five years in Wyoming, Montana, the Dakota Territories, and Nebraska during the Indian Wars of 1872 to 1877. His enlistment papers show him to be 6-feet, 2-inches with gray eyes and brown hair. No mention of his scar or head condition were noted by the recruiting officer, Capt. Frank Aben of the 4th Cavalry. The date was October 14, 1872. He and a friend posed for a photograph in Cheyenne, Wyoming, shortly after the enlistment, and the scar across his forehead is very noticeable. Men were in short supply out West, and recruitment officers had a quota to fill, so a scar was not a bother.

In his 257-page diary, George records in detail his travels out West, and the adventures he experienced over a five-year period. He met members of the Shoshone, Sioux, and Cheyenne Nations and witnessed the final destruction of a native way of life. Toward the back of his diary, he lists medical cures for common illnesses. His daughter said these cures were given to him by Sitting Bull, a famous medicine man and chief, but there is no way to authenticate this report as no written reports of this exchange were ever found.

Upon arriving in Cheyenne, Wyoming, in late October 1872 by Union Pacific Railroad, George spent four to five days riding to Fort Laramie on horseback. He was listed on regimental rolls as a new recruit at Fort Laramie on November 1, 1872.

George S. Howard spent a majority of his enlistment at this most famous of Western outposts and the rest of his time was divided between other isolated posts from Fort Fetterman in Wyoming to Omaha Barracks in Nebraska. He never stayed at other outposts longer than a few months and often spent months camping along Western rivers far from any fort. His greatest pleasure was hunting and fishing for big game and trout by the arm- and horse-full.

His daughter said that his excellent sense of direction and ability to communicate with the Indians provided him the opportunity to become a scout and hunter for his unit throughout his enlistment. Additionally, he guided wagon trains from Fort Laramie on the Oregon Trail past Register Rock and Laramie Peak and escorted lumber trains to and from sawmills near Laramie Peak.

He and his best friend, who remains nameless, enjoyed the bounty of fresh game from Laramie Valley to the mountains outside of Yellowstone National Park, a park established on March 1, 1872.

When George arrived at Fort Laramie as a private in the fall of 1872, he was assigned construction projects. Regimental reports list him as active as a carpenter and guide throughout his stay at the fort, which lasted until the fall of 1874. Monthly reports filed by his commanding officers, and preserved on microfilm at the National Archives, match George's poetry and prose, although his accounts provide the emotion lacking in the officer's writings.

George was listed as an escort for a detachment of troops to the Red Cloud Agency in late July of 1873. Throughout the fall of 1873, George's company and Company K of the 2nd Cavalry scouted for Indians by horse from Fort Laramie to Fort Fetterman for a distance of over 763 miles. They scouted the country north of Laramie Peak and explored La Bonte and Horseshoe Creeks.

During this same time period, they crossed creeks and canyons in the vicinity of Wind River, Cottonwood Creek, Horse Creek, and Shoshone River where George and his unnamed friend hunted for deer, antelope, and elk. Once he came upon a group of grizzly and left his deer meat for them to feast upon in South Park.

Much of George's time in 1873 was spent escorting lumber trains to and from Laramie Peak and scouting for Indians at the same time. He expresses great wonderment at the bounty of game available in Wyoming, Montana, and South Dakota.

George and a detachment of Company E left the fort on September 11, 1873, for the purpose of "scouting and ascertaining the practicality of a wagon route through the Black Hills in the vicinity of Collier," according to regimental reports. They concluded that such a route could be taken through the Laramie Plains, but it was impractical for general travel. The group returned from the exploration via Laramie Peak and Cottonwood Canyon on September 18, having traveled 152 miles.

Wind River in northwestern Wyoming where George S. Howard and his hunting partner traveled in 1872 and 1873 on their way to the Yellowstone area near present-day Cody, Wyoming.

George passed many sandstone outcrops as shown in this 1876 photograph at Crow Butte near Camp Robinson, Nebraska. George was at Camp Robinson and the Red Cloud Agency in 1875 and 1876. The camp was established in 1874.

Photograph courtesy of National Archives.

Just beyond the boundaries of Fort Laramie, George S. Howard recorded seeing Indian lodges. Pictured are some of the lodges near the post in the early 1870s.

Photograph courtesy of National Archives.

Fort Laramie in 1876 was the staging area for many campaigns during the Indian Wars. George was stationed there from 1872 to 1874 and traveled in and out of the post from 1875 to 1877. Most of the buildings were painted barn red as this was the most available color.

Photograph by John Reneau.

"Old Bedlam" was the name soldiers gave the bachelor officers' quarters at Fort Laramie as it was the site of many wild parties. The building is fully restored and open to visitors throughout the year.

In October 1873, Company E traveled north of Laramie Peak to the Horseshoe Creek and returned to Fort Laramie by October 15. Company E was asked to scout between Scotts Bluff and Horse Creek in late December and marched to Lawrence and the Old Red Cloud Agency by Christmas. After covering 163 miles in two weeks, the company returned to Fort Laramie December 27, 1873.

Companies E and K were employed during the month of February 1874 as escorts for wagon trains going to sawmills at Laramie Peak and in scouting after Indians through the Valley of Laramie to Phillips Ranch, Upper Crossing, Horseshoe Creek, and La Bonte Creek on the Fetterman Road. George was listed as repairing telegraph wire, scouting, and escorting trains to sawmills.

George was selected to be on a detachment of Company E troops that left the post for the Spotted Tail Agency on September 9, 1874, to participate in a surveying team that explored the northern line of Nebraska to the northwestern section of the state. The team returned to Fort Laramie September 30, after covering 306 miles. He was a scout for this exploration party.

Sometime in 1874, work began on a new bridge across the North Platte River within two miles of Fort Laramie. George was listed as helping to construct a bridge, so one can only assume that the bridge was this famous structure.

The Fort Laramie Bridge stands today crossing a mild-mannered North Platte, but in 1874, the waterway was violent and turbulent. The bridge became a critical link to the Black Hills of the Dakota Territories and provided a safe crossing for settlers and miners who traveled along the Cheyenne and Deadwood Route. This was the road considered the best to reach the gold fields of the Black Hills.

Because of its durability and strategic location, the bridge influenced the establishment of the famous Cheyenne and Black Hills Stage and Express Line. The bridge remained in use until 1958. Today, it stands as a historical monument to the expansion of white settlers and the destruction of the Indian way of life. Walking across the bridge after reading George's diary brought a sense of connection to a soldier's life 120 years ago.

One event in 1874 made a lasting impression on the young scout. On February 9, two soldiers, Lt. Levi Herbert Robinson of the 14th Infantry, and Corp. James Coleman of Company K, 2nd Cavalry, were tortured and killed by Indians while hunting for antelope near Laramie Peak. They had been escorts for a lumber train from the sawmills and had decided to hunt for game.

George and a small detachment of soldiers were ordered to recover the arrow-riddled and decomposed bodies in the bluffs 38 miles north of Fort Laramie. George describes in detail how the men were killed, and said he was assigned the "melancholy task" of recovery. Robinson was a popular junior officer who arrived at Fort Laramie in December of 1872, one month after George Howard arrived.

George's revelation of the details about these deaths may be the only complete description of the body recovery. The complete file of Lt. Robinson does not exist at Fort Robinson Historic Site, even though the curator thoroughly examined his records. Robinson's remains were supposedly received by his pregnant widow, Mary Darling Robinson of Vermont, at Fort Laramie just after February 14, 1874. His widow escorted the body back East in May.

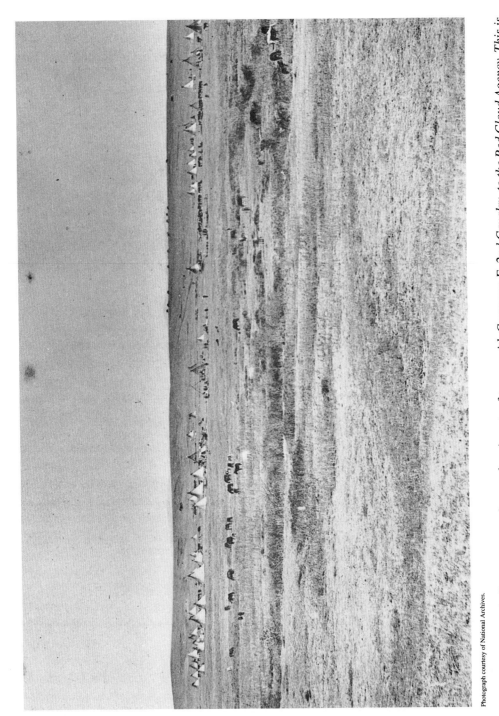

From 1872 to 1874, George escorted several regiments of troops with Company E, 2nd Cavalry, to the Red Cloud Agency. This is an Indian encampment near the agency in 1876.

According to military records, Corp. Coleman's body was buried February 9, at Fort Laramie. George and his company, along with members of Company K, were assigned the task of scouting for the forty to fifty Indians involved in the attack. George and a handful of other scouts carried the bodies back to Fort Laramie.

Shortly after the February incident, a Sioux expedition was organized with 972 men involving companies from the 3rd Cavalry and companies from the 8th, 13th, and 14th Infantries. Companies of the 2nd Cavalry, including George's unit, were assigned to Fort Laramie under the command of Maj. E. M. Baker.

Fort Laramie played an important part in the life of George S. Howard. The fort was a bustling post in 1874 consisting of several long, wooden barracks for enlisted men, nine homes for officers, including the two-story bachelors' quarters fondly called "Old Bedlam," a trader's store, band quarters, a hospital, several stables for horses and mules and assorted buildings for fort activities such as baking and eating. No fence or stockade surrounded this open-air fort except the trout-filled flowing waters of the Laramie River.

A map, drawn in 1874, shows cavalry barracks across the Laramie River from the main portion of the fort. These barracks were close to the horse and mule stables and the fort laundress. Today nothing remains of the barracks where George lived from 1872 to 1874, but he told his wife and daughters he enjoyed nights of reading and writing beside the stream.

Fort Laramie was first established as Fort William in 1834 by William Sublette, William Anderson, and William Patton as a fur trading post with the Cheyenne and Sioux bands. The fort became the starting point for many military operations and attracted settlers who planned to make their way on the Oregon Trail beginning in the 1840s. The military fort of Laramie was established on August 12, 1849, by Maj. Winslow F. Sanderson after the U.S. Army purchased the land from Brice Husband who represented the Northwestern Fur Company, according to Crofutt's 1878 *New Overland Tourist and Pacific Coast Guide*.

Fort Laramie is situated 89 miles north from Cheyenne on the left bank of the Laramie River, about two miles from its junction with the North Platte, and on the Overland Road to Oregon and California. The fort consisted of 54 miles of flat, open prairie. Much of George's writings were done along the Laramie River facing the parade grounds that exist today.

Besides fishing, George's greatest pleasure was reading and writing. The fort had a modest library filled with newspapers, novels, and magazines of the period. Library records at the fort state that as of 1868 more than 300 volumes, mostly religious and military in nature, were available for enlisted men to check out and study. George enjoyed carrying his "library" with him into the field to read after camp had been made.

An 1879 memo from the post librarian lists such periodicals as *Atlantic Monthly*, *Harper's Weekly*, and the *Chicago Times*. A post assistant librarian was hired at 20 cents a day on December 3, 1868, indicating that extra help was needed to maintain the collection. The entire post library was transferred to Fort Robinson in 1889.

At Register Cliff, thousands of Western travelers etched their names in the white sandstone cliffs before turning their attention to uncharted territory and the gold fields of California. Wagon ruts embedded in the rock remain today as testimony to their activity. Deep wagon ruts can be seen today in the sandstone and hardened mud near the cliffs facing Laramie Peak where George guided them.

In May of 1874, Company E escorted Maj. Thaddeus H. Stanton, future chief of scouts under Gen. George Crook during the Big Horn and Sioux Expeditions of 1876 and paymaster general of the Army, to the Red Cloud and Whetstone Agencies for a total of 203 miles by horseback, crossing the creeks of Bone, Chattering, Rawhide, White, and Running Waters. Much of this trip was in present-day South Dakota.

The Whetstone Agency was established on May 10, 1870, on the right bank of the Missouri River about 30 miles northwest of Fort Randall in present-day South Dakota to protect settlers and white troops against the Sioux. This land is now a part of the Rosebud Indian Reservation where Smithsonian intern Terry Gray, who helped with research on the diary, teaches at Sinte Gleska College. The agency never became a fort and was abandoned in 1872, but cavalry units still referred to it as a stopping point throughout the 1876 campaigns.

In the summer, George and his company continued to escort log and wagon trains into the mountains. George was assigned to assist in a surveying expedition along the northern border of Nebraska to the northwest area of the state in September, and returned with his company September 30, having traveled 306 miles.

Throughout George's stay at Fort Laramie, lumber from Laramie Peak sawmills was transported back to the post to construct a new cavalry barracks that were completed in 1874. George used his carpentry skills to work on construction projects. He was also listed as an escort for wagon trains carrying lumber to the fort. It can only be concluded that he helped with the construction of the new barracks that remain today in a fully restored condition, complete with the furniture and soldier's equipment and uniforms from that time. George left Fort Laramie before his company stayed in this building.

Late in the fall of 1874, Company E was transferred from Fort Laramie to Omaha Barracks, Nebraska, and remained at the barracks outside the City of Omaha until May 5, 1875. Omaha Barracks, established in 1868 on the right bank of the Missouri River, was constructed to guard the Western frontier from Indian attacks and to provide winter quarters for troops not needed on the Plains.

Illustrations of the post in *Crofutt's Trans-Continental Tourist's* guide book of 1872 show it to be a sprawling 80-acre compound within sight of the city. At Omaha Barracks, George developed many relationships with women and finds comfort in their companionship even though several marriage engagements ended in failure. He lists their names in his diary and several of the women write messages on the pages of his book identifying themselves as citizens of Omaha.

A road from the city to the barracks provided easy access for the citizens and soldiers, according to the tourist guide. The City of Omaha in 1877 boasted four daily newspapers, two colleges, fifteen churches, five banks, many hotels, and the ever-popular distilleries and breweries of alcoholic spirits. For someone like George, who had grown accustomed to frostbite and sacrifice, life at Omaha Barracks must have been considered a vacation from the hardships of Plains living.

Springtime in 1875 brought new movements for Company E and George. The unit returned to the Plains and marched to Camp Sheridan by way of Camp Robinson. They arrived in Camp Sheridan on May 22, 1875, having marched 241 miles. Camp Robinson was a mile

The gold rush in the Black Hills began in 1875 when fortune seekers poured into the sacred hunting grounds of the Indians. Here, miners pan for gold on Deadwood Creek in the Dakota Territories in 1876. The photograph is by Stanley J. Morrow.

and a half from the Red Cloud Agency near the White River in northwestern Nebraska near present-day Crawford.

The activities of the Red Cloud Agency and Camp Robinson blended after 1874 when it was renamed to honor Lt. Levi Robinson who was killed by Indians near Fort Laramie and whose body was recovered by George Howard and a company of scouts in February of 1874. This camp was also the headquarters for the Pine Ridge Agency. It became Fort Robinson in 1878 and was abandoned in 1948 to become Fort Robinson State Park and Museum.

Camp Sheridan was slightly north of Robinson at the Spotted Tail Agency near the border of Nebraska and South Dakota. The camp was established on March 12, 1874, near the original site of the Spotted Tail Agency on the east or right bank of the West Fork of Beaver Creek about 12 miles above the junction of the White River in present-day Sheridan County, Wyoming. Camp Sheridan, named for the famous Civil War general, was abandoned in May of 1881. It was established to protect the Brule Sioux, according to Robert Roberts in his book, *Encyclopedia of Historic Forts*. Both were barren outposts that lacked the entertainment and comforts of the Omaha Barracks or home.

By fall of 1875, George was listed in company reports as a sergeant working to find miners in the Black Hills of the Dakotas. He was based at Camp Collier, Dakota Territories, an Army site that was about 100 miles south of Deadwood in present-day South Dakota. Throughout the fall, George patrolled the Black Hills in search of miners and arrived at Fort Sanders, Wyoming Territory, after traveling 300 miles. He and a detachment of men from Company E, under the command of Capt. Elijah R. Wells, delivered eight miners to the fort on September 21.

The onslaught of domestication continued when rich deposits of gold were found on Harney's Peak by Col. George Armstrong Custer and his men during the Black Hills Expedition of 1874. A gold rush began in earnest in 1875 when Professor Walter Jenny confirmed Custer's report in May of that year, and a steady stream of miners flooded the sacred hunting grounds of the Indians, causing great unrest. The towns of Deadwood and Custer City exploded in population and services. The principal wealth of the region for white men were quartz mines that numbered 742 by 1878. From the influx of miners came farmers, merchants, and all types of professional services that George enjoyed when he stayed in Deadwood.

George mentions Camp Collins as the site of Custer City. In Watson Parker's book, *Gold in the Black Hills*, the camp and city are identified as one in the same. Capt. Edwin Pollock established Camp Collins to control the activities of miners and provide services for soldiers. He arrived from Fort Laramie in the fall of 1875 with troops from the 9th Infantry and the 2nd and 3rd Cavalry. Headquarters of the camp were set up in a log cabin. The troops arrested dozens of miners, confined them to quarters in Custer City, and sent them to Fort Laramie where the miners were eventually released, according to Parker. Gold mining was a great temptation to soldiers who received meager wages, and Pollock soon found his men deserting in droves.

By November of 1875, Pollock's troops, including George Howard, left Custer City and Camp Collins for Wyoming, and the population of miners swelled from 500 in December 1875 to 4,000 miners in January 1876.

Somewhere in this sea of canvas tents, taken in February of 1876, is Sgt. George S. Howard, who assembled for the start of the Big Horn Expedition with hundreds of other soldiers. Buildings at Fort Fetterman are shown on the hill overlooking the North Platte River. The scene looks much the same today, complete with an abundance of jackrabbits and butterflies.

The United States government offered money to the Indians to compensate them for the mining by white men on sacred hunting grounds, but such offers were refused by the chiefs. A treaty had been signed by Indian chiefs and white generals at Fort Laramie in 1868 that was supposed to protect the hunting grounds from white miners, ranchers, and farmers that streamed into the Black Hills. To the disgust of the Indian leaders, most of the hunting grounds were not included in a proposed Sioux reservation mentioned in the 1868 agreement.

Gen. George Crook and cavalry escorts were assigned to keep the peace and maintain order. The cavalry patrols did not work, and by the end of 1875 uncontrolled numbers of white men arrived in the Black Hills to harvest its riches of minerals, timber, and soil. George S. Howard was one of those cavalry soldiers who patrolled the miners' activities and tried to keep the peace. Deadwood was a common stopping point for George and his company to relax and resupply their unit.

Fort Sanders, where George arrived in the fall of 1875, was located six and a half miles from Red Buttes and two and one half miles from the city of Laramie on the railroad line. The fort consisted of log and stone buildings and one wooden frame structure that served as the post's headquarters. The fort was established on June 23, 1866, by two companies of the 3rd Battalion under the command of Brevet Lt. Col. H. M. Mizner, a captain in the 18th Infantry. It was at this fort that George met several ladies who lived in Laramie, and he enjoyed the attractions of this small Plains town.

With a population of 4,000, Laramie contained the finer comforts of home for George. Trees lined many of the streets, and families from a variety of nationalities constructed frame houses. Crofutt's 1878 tourist guide said Laramie contained "the spirit of improvement with the completion of numerous stores, hotels, banks, churches, schools, dwellings, and a court house and jail." A road through town had just been completed when George arrived, and a favorite entertainment spot was the newly constructed Laramie Hotel beside the train station. A daily and weekly newspaper, *The Sentinel*, added to George's enjoyment of Laramie "civilization." George fell in love with Elizabeth "Lizzie" Stevens in Laramie, but their engagement broke up just before he returned to New Hampshire in 1877.

George describes the grassy beauty of the Laramie Plains that extended north from Laramie City and Fort Sanders. Cattle ranching was the dominate industry. Crofutt's 1878 tourist guide reported 90,000 head of cattle, 85,000 head of sheep, and 3,000 horses and mules within forty miles of Laramie City that carried a market value of $2.2 million.

The ancient and massive buffalo herds were gone by the time George arrived, but he mentions large buffalo herds and hunts farther north towards Yellowstone. In a span of ten years, from 1867 to 1877 when George left the Plains, livestock populations grew from 500 head in 1867 to a quarter of a million head.

Moccasin Joe during the Big Horn and Sioux Expedition

George remained with his company at Fort Sanders, Wyoming Territory, throughout December 1875 and January 1876 performing regular garrison duties. Then, in February 1876, Companies E and C left Fort Sanders and headed for Fort Fetterman to await further orders.

Brig. Gen. George Crook, famous Indian fighter and Civil War hero, was not greatly respected by Sgt. George S. Howard. Sgt. Howard thought the Big Horn Expedition was handled improperly and battles were fought poorly. Here, Gen. Crook is shown in 1876 as he would have appeared to George during the Big Horn Expedition. Gen. Crook was called "Natan Lupan" (The Great Chief Gray Wolf) and "Wicakpi Yamini" (Three Stars) by the Sioux, Shoshone, and Cheyenne.

Martha Canary Burke, known as Calamity Jane, served as a scout and teamster for Gen. George Crook's 1876 expedition when she was 23. She died in 1903 at age 53 and was buried in Deadwood, Dakota Territories. This photograph was taken close to the time she served as an army teamster.

George records the campaign of 1876 in prose and poetry from this point, and details his thoughts as massive numbers of cavalry and infantry troops arrived at Fort Fetterman for the start of the famous Big Horn Expedition.

President Ulysses S. Grant had ordered all Indians onto reservations by January 31, 1876, or be subjected to military action. Frustrated by the influx of settlers and miners and the breakdown in negotiations with white men, Indians had begun to attack ranches along the Union Pacific Railroad in the North Platte Valley. These attacks stimulated the United States government to begin the military build-up at Fort Fetterman.

Fort Fetterman, built in 1867, was the last Army post established along the Indian border. Plain plank and adobe buildings sprinkled on the barren landscape of this 40-acre fort made this post one of the least favorite of all assignments for the Plains soldier. The Bozeman Trail wound a long, twisting northwesterly route to the Montana gold fields from Fort Fetterman, and a telegraph line to Fort Reno was established during the time George camped there.

The fort was named in honor of Brevet Lt. Col. William J. Fetterman, a captain in the 18th Infantry, who was killed during the Fort Phil Kearny massacre of December 21, 1866. The fort is located on the south side of the North Platte River, 135 miles from Cheyenne, 90 miles south of Fort Reno, and 70 miles northwest of Fort Laramie. It remained operational until 1882. The town of Douglas sprang up less than ten miles south of the original fort site in 1886, so the usefulness of Fort Fetterman declined.

The buildings of the old fort were destroyed, dismantled or moved to other locations in the 1880s and remained in disrepair until the Wyoming Museums and Historical Department took an interest in the site and restored the original officers' quarters and ordnance warehouse. Today, a museum tracing the history and activity of the fort is contained in the officers' headquarter building and is open to the public May 15 to Labor Day.

As the troops assembled along the Platte River below Fort Fetterman's lookout ridge in 1876, singers and dancers from the saloons across the river created distractions. These saloons sprang up at most military posts and were called "Hog Ranches." The "Hog Ranch" just outside the boundaries of Fort Fetterman was one of the most notorious in the region. Soldiers swam the river to reach the entertainment. George was one of hundreds of cavalry and infantry soldiers assembled below Fort Fetterman in the winter and early spring of 1876. He claimed he did not drink in a letter to his mother back home. No one knows, however, if he partook of the festivities at the "Hog Ranch."

It was at Fort Fetterman that Martha Canary "Calamity Jane" Burke joined the expedition as a guide and mule team driver at the age of 23. She was also rumored to have been a singer at the "Hog Ranch" near Fort Fetterman, according to modern-day curator Stanley Lash whose grandfather was the fort's blacksmith in the 1870s and 1880s. She was 23 at the time of the Big Horn Expedition and was discovered to be a woman in camp below Fort Fetterman. The rumor of her discovery spread like wildfire among the restless troops, Lash said.

The first encounter with Indians for George took place a short trip from Fort Fetterman on the Powder River in March of 1876. Portions of George's diary are of special interest to historians studying the Battle of Powder River as it provides a cavalry scout's perspective on the events leading up to and throughout the skirmish with the Sioux. George's account of the battle is found in Chapters Three and Four of this book.

J. W. Vaughn, in his book, *The Reynolds Campaign on Powder River*, considers the Battle of Powder River to be one of the most important events in Western history, for it marked the beginning of the end for those bands of Indians who opposed the tide of white settlement. George S. Howard was so profoundly influenced by this battle and his commanding officer, Col. Joseph J. Reynolds, that he periodically used "Joe Reynolds" as a pen name throughout his diary entries following the battle date of March 17, 1876.

The War Department received authority to take action against hostiles on February 7, 1876, and to follow the plans of Gen. Philip H. Sheridan, commander of the Division of the Missouri and Civil War hero. Brig. Gen. George Crook was ordered to lead troops north to Powder River country from Fort Fetterman, Wyoming Territory; hence, the references in George Howard's diary that his company left Fetterman.

George S. Howard's Company E entered Fort Fetterman from Fort Sanders, Wyoming Territory, on February 27, and Col. Reynolds issued general orders on that day to form the Big Horn Expedition. Six battalions of cavalry and infantry left Fort Fetterman March 1, 1876, including George and Company E, 2nd Cavalry, under the command of Capt. Alexander Moore.

George notes that on the second night out from Fort Fetterman the first of four Indian raids took place. On March 3, at 2 a.m., a cattle rancher, John Wright, was shot through the lung. Fifty live cattle, for the purpose of feeding the troops, were stampeded by the Indians and lost on the plains. George talks of great hardships. One hardship was the loss of fresh meat on March 3.

Moccasin Joe notes the expedition crossed the Powder River to Old Fort Reno. Lt. John G. Bourke, the aide to Gen. Crook, mentions in his diary that, upon crossing the ice cold waters of the Powder River, the soldiers entered the ruins. Fort Reno was established August 14, 1865, on a ridge some fifty feet above the left bank of the Powder River and about four miles below the mouth of Dry Fork as a protection to miners and settlers who traveled the Bozeman Trail. Today, the ruins remain as they were in 1868 about 22 miles from present-day Kaycee, Wyoming.

Fort Reno was established by Brig. Gen. Patrick E. Connor and was abandoned on August 16, 1868, after the signing of the Fort Laramie Treaty with the Sioux and Cheyenne Nations on April 29, 1868. Sioux warriors burned the fort and a smaller establishment, Fort McKinney, was created three miles south of Fort Reno in October of 1876 after the Big Horn Expedition.

Troops on their march during the Big Horn Expedition of 1876 made camp on March 6, at 4 p.m. on the banks of Crazy Woman's Fork. By March 7, the troops began to prepare for active combat. George notes that on this day pack mules were used to carry supplies. Gen. Crook left the wagon trains of supplies with the infantry and used pack mules because the terrain became so treacherous. George writes that they traveled along the Clear Creek Fork of the Powder River. Army records state that the expedition camped on Clear Fork March 8.

During the night, the first of several harsh snowstorms which George wrote about, began. With few food rations, blankets, or shelter, it was little wonder Sgt. Howard remembers this march as being "one of the most severe Trips I have heard of."

Near the Tongue River, the soldiers, mules, and horses had great trouble traveling over icy trails. Eighteen times the expedition crossed the frozen waters of the Tongue River on March 12, according to the news dispatches of Robert A. Strahorn, reporter for the *Rocky Mountain News*, of Denver, Colorado. Strahorn's dispatches, sent to his newspaper March 22, record in great detail the extent of hardships the soldiers endured and provide additional information about the march and battle not made clear in George's diary accounts in poetry and prose.

In George's diary, he says the soldiers made two night marches on March 16 and 17. According to Frank Grouard, special scout to Gen. Crook, Crook issued orders for a forced night march on the 16th because Grouard had spotted Indians near the expedition and feared Indians on the Powder River would discover the troops and leave the area before a fight.

Frank Grouard and his 15 scouts saw a hunting party of two Cheyenne Indians and chased them away from the expedition in a northeasterly direction toward Powder River. George S. Howard was one of those scouts, based upon his poetry entries in the diary. He tells of the discovery of the two Indians on Otter Creek which was where the scouts traveled to locate the Indians.

Crook instructed Reynolds to find the Indian village, thought to be that of the famous and feared Sioux warrior, Crazy Horse. George's company, along with Companies M, E, and F of the 3rd Cavalry, and Companies E and I of the 2nd Cavalry left camp on Otter Creek on the evening of March 16, after enjoying a hearty dinner. Crook commanded Reynolds to capture the Indian pony herd and to do as much damage to the village as possible. Crook claimed later that he asked Reynolds to take meat and provisions from the village to give to the freezing and starving soldiers.

After the battle, and during the court martial proceedings against Reynolds and two other officers, Reynolds claimed he was not ordered to take the meat and provisions, but had been ordered to destroy everything.

Moccasin Joe discusses the forced march and battle, giving heartrending details of the conditions the men endured. Mr. Strahorn's dispatch on March 18, after the march and battle that was found in the Library of Congress reads:

> "Without doubt, the most remarkable event of Gen. Crook's present campaign was the night march commenced early on the evening of the 16th. As a matter of history it well deserves a place by the side of any similar incident known to frontier service; and if the three hundred gallant and uncomplaining spirits who participate in its thrilling scenes had nothing more . . . to tell . . . this would be enough."

The scouts under the leadership of Frank Grouard tracked the two Indian hunters up the north branch of Otter Creek to its head and then crossed a divide in the valley of the Powder River, according to J. W. Vaughn in his book, *The Reynolds Campaign on Powder River*. Intense cold and wind hampered the movement of the scouts and soldiers. Reynolds reported

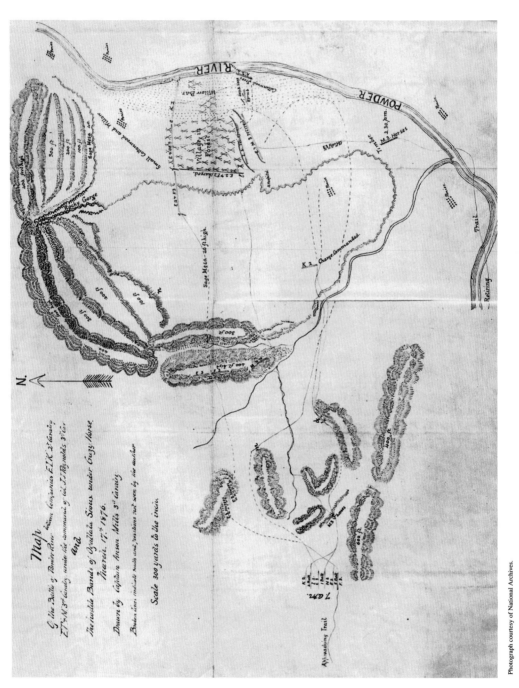

This map, drawn by Capt. Anson Mills of the 3rd Cavalry, was found in his personnel file at the National Archives. It shows the troop movements and Indian locations during the Battle of Powder River on March 17, 1876. Sgt. Howard wrote three poems regarding the Powder River incident.

that on March 12, at 8 a.m., the thermometer reading was 26 degrees below zero. The scouts went ahead while the soldiers waited and rested in a ravine six miles from the Indian village. The scouts returned to the cavalry at 7 a.m., March 17, and the march continued. George's diary entries detail the encampment and march in blinding snow.

Under the command of 1st Lt. W. C. Rawolle, George's Company E led the 300 soldiers to the foot of a mountain overlooking the Indian village the cavalry had sought since March 1, when they left Fetterman. George mentions in one of his poems Big Panther Mountain which most likely was the mountain the troops climbed on March 17, prior to the battle.

The 5th Battalion, under the command of Capt. Moore, was assigned to go down the valley of Thompson Creek and stop before the Indians (consisting of Northern Cheyenne, and Oglala and Minneconjoux Sioux) sighted the men. Grouard guided the 5th Battalion into position. The companies under Capt. Henry Noyes and Capt. James Egan were to drive the pony herd of 800 animals toward Capt. Moore's waiting men.

As the 5th Battalion arrived at the designated position, Reynolds realized they were too far from the Indian village. The battalion was moved 600 yards northeast of and across Thompson Creek. George's Company E lined a wooded ridge next to Capt. Moore's Company F and watched the village from a thousand yards. Lt. Rawolle was advised to move into a better location. Company E then moved 300 yards closer to the village, remaining camouflaged in the bushes. George S. Howard writes about the juggling for position and the movement of the troops in his first poem about the Powder River battle.

The attacking column of soldiers, composed of the companies of Capt. Egan and Capt. Noyes, took over an hour to begin the charge because the horses and men struggled over the rugged series of ravines and gulches as described in Vaughn's book. The 5th Battalion watched as Noyes and Egan led the charge at 9:05 a.m., March 17. Forty-seven men took part in the charge as noted by George in his poem. As the charge took place and Indians, cavalry soldiers and ponies became entangled in battle, George S. Howard's company joined eight men from Capt. Moore's company and started down the westerly bluffs to join the soldiers in the field.

Because George's Company E had great trouble moving down the bluffs, Rawolle led the company on a detour which further delayed his men from entering the village. During all the confusion on the bluffs and in the village, some of the Indians herded 200 ponies away from the battle. Reynolds had left 90 men to tend to the cavalry horses, since most of the soldiers were fighting on foot. That left only 210 men fighting 200 Indians. Reynolds realized his troops could not do damage, so he gave orders to burn everything in the 105 teepees and to retreat as quickly as possible.

While Rawolle's men, including George, entered the village, Indians started firing on them from the northerly bluffs; and as ponies from the main herd ran past the soldiers, two sergeants (Howard and Land), and Pvt. Pat Douglas were ordered to recapture 15 to 20 ponies while under severe fire from the Indians. When the ponies were recaptured, Rawolle's men entered the village and by 10:30 a.m. most of the village structures and supplies had been destroyed. The Indians had escaped to the bluffs in safety.

Soldiers rest on a rock following the Battle of Slim Buttes in the Dakota Territories.

Reynolds ordered the cavalry horses to be brought to the men in the village, but because 90 men and horses were on the ridge, it took two hours for the horses to be brought. During this time period, four soldiers were killed and six to seven others were wounded, including Rawolle. George was in the frenzy and noted that dead and dying soldiers were left on the battlefield, much to his dismay.

George wondered how a commanding officer such as Reynolds could do such a thing and why the village with all its supplies was destroyed when men were dying of frostbite and starvation. Cavalry records note that 66 men were treated for frostbite by the camp doctor. George and the other men were ordered to rid themselves of their heavy overcoats before the march, adding to the extreme discomfort. George said his feet were especially numb.

A rare map, drawn by Capt. Anson Mills of the 3rd Cavalry and preserved in his personnel files at the National Archives, shows the movement of troops and the location of the Indian village that was attacked. This map may be the only illustration of the Battle of Powder River. The minute details illustrated on this hand-drawn map show exact locations of all the troops, including George's Company E, and provided me with the information needed to trace George's footsteps during the battle. A photograph of the map is reproduced in this section of the book.

Much to the continued disgust of the cavalry soldiers, the 700 captured Indian ponies were herded up Lodgepole Creek during the retreat and left unattended overnight, based on orders by Reynolds. Forty or fifty angry Indians followed the retreating column of troops and ponies and recaptured the herd March 18. The returning troops expected to be greeted by Crook, but to their dismay, no column of supplies and fresh troops were on Otter Creek as had been planned before Reynolds and his troops left on the forced on March 16.

The next morning, the herd was sighted two or three miles from camp on some bluffs. Crook, after rejoining the troops, was angry at Reynolds for not sending troops to recapture the herd. The loss of the herd and the destruction of supplies was a major point against Reynolds when court proceedings began in 1877.

Reynolds was found guilty in a military court of law for leaving dead on the battlefield in the hands of the enemy, failing to make any attempt to recapture escaped ponies and mules, and conducting himself as was unbecoming an officer and a gentleman. Capt. Alexander Moore and Capt. Henry E. Noyes were also court-martialled for their conduct in this battle.

Volumes of information regarding the charges and the officers' trial are located in their personnel files stored at the National Archives. After George writes the poetry about the battle, he often signs entries in his journal as "Joseph Reynolds."

George was obsessed with the slaughter of the Indian women and children at the village and found great comfort in his poems that expressed his disgust. He didn't think much of the commanding officers, including Gen. Crook.

George was one of the soldiers who participated in the Battle of the Rosebud (June 17, 1876) and the Battle of Slim Buttes (September 9, 1876). He was one of hundreds of men who was forced to eat mule and horse meat in September of 1876 when supplies ran out in the Black Hills during the famous Starvation March.

George arrived at Fort Sanders with his company on November 5, 1876, and remained at the post performing regular garrison duties until he was discharged on May 31, 1877. He returned by railroad to Hinsdale, New Hampshire, following his service in the 2nd Cavalry.

George S. Howard's daily diary entries in Chapter Three of this book record his military action from April of 1876 to November of 1876, details not found in the regimental rolls. On the microfilm in the National Archives, months go by without reports from the commanding officer. One can assume that field conditions were so harsh that monthly reports were not received or even filed, which makes George's personal entries so significant.

How did George preserve this journal as he rode from battle to battle? How did George keep the diary from getting wet? Where did he store the diary when he was not in camp? These questions will always remain a mystery. We know from his daughter that he used the diary as a pillow, so he must have carried it into the field throughout his enlistment. Based upon his notations in the margins of the diary, we guess that his daily entries in 1876 may have been recorded in a small log book and transcribed when he returned to his barracks at Fort Sanders or to his home in New England.

The bulk of the 257-page diary written in a ledger book contains his poetry and prose that reflect his innermost thoughts as he survived the conditions of the Plains before extensive white settlement had begun. The poems of his battles, guard duties, lost loves, and found comforts capture his spirit and his deepest thoughts.

The scar across the forehead of George S. Howard (left) can be clearly seen in this 1874 tintype as he posed with a best friend, his "bunky" and "pard." Although George often mentions his dear friend in poems, George never identified him by name.

Chapter Two

Home to Marriage and Murder

George returned to his mother's home in Hinsdale, New Hampshire, in the summer of 1877 to help run the family boardinghouse. Later, George met his future wife, Martha Colburn, who was a boarder in his mother's house. Martha was learning to become a tailor. The intense courtship lasted a year.

On January 22, 1879, George and Martha were married in Hinsdale by the Rev. H. H. Hamilton, according to their marriage certificate found in George S. Howard's personnel files in the National Archives. One year later, Bessie May was born, and a year after that, in 1881, Grace was born.

Life with George was not pleasant, based upon the letters from Grace. She wrote in 1977 at age 96:

> "After marriage they went to Greenfield, Massachusetts, to live. . . . There was a great railroad yard there and that is where my father worked. Not too long after, he commenced to act erratically, but one did not know why. He soon was transferred to the Fitchburg yards, they being a little less hectic than the one in Greenfield. Then he began to be away from home. Sometimes two days, sometimes more. He did not know where he had been.
>
> "One time the circus came to Fitchburg and it was found he left with the circus and was gone a week. Of course anyone special in the circus had accommodations in a car especially for them, but the workers could sleep anywhere. He was sleeping on top of one of the cars (they were drawn up on the flatcars). The train jolted, and he received a blow to the head and came home. Then he began to have terrible headaches, could not sleep nights and often walked all night."

George wandered into the Fitchburg railroad yard one night when he was having one of his fits. This would be the end of him. The *Fitchburg Sentinel* ran a story on page 3 of the January 18, 1887, edition which told of his death. Less than ten years after returning from the West, and after surviving the hardships of frontier life, George S. Howard, Moccasin Joe, was dead.

The *Fitchburg Sentinel* carried the following article:

> "An unfortunate shooting affair occurred on River Street about 1:30 a.m., today (January 18, 1887). The victim was a railroad man named George S. Howard, who

Bessie May Howard, left, and Grace Howard, right, were the only children of George S. and Martha Howard. This photograph was taken about 1885 in Hinsdale, New Hampshire, about two years before George was murdered. The girls were four and five years old at the time.

boarded at the Citizens' House, and his wife, to whom he was married eight years ago, and two daughters, six and seven years of age, respectively, living in Shirley. *[At the time of the shooting, George and Martha were separated due to strain in the marriage caused from his mental illness.]*

He was formerly employed as conductor on the western division of the Fitchburg railroad and had previously been a brakeman on a passenger train. He was serving in that capacity on the train which left the rail and went through the wooden bridge near Pequoig in Athol, June 16, 1870, when George A. Johnson of this city and several other persons were killed. Mr. Howard had his skull fractured and has never fully recovered from the effects of that accident.

"He has for about four years been troubled with epileptic fits and at times acted in a peculiar manner. He has recently been employed in the Fitchburg railroad car shop in this city, his liability to fits making it unsafe for him to work on a train. He had not been at work for several days previous to the shooting. He is a large man (230 to 250 pounds, six feet, two inches, muscular) and his shopmates say he frequently carried a large knife which he was rather fond of showing. He was at the railroad shop Monday, and his shopmates say that he behaved strangely.

"As (Police) Officer Michael M. Connor was coming down River Street, and was on the railroad crossing, Howard came from behind a car and followed the officer till opposite the first house east of the crossing, when Howard asked the time. Connor took out his watch, when Howard seized the watch and struck Connor twice.

"As Connor reeled back he drew his revolver and fired and the ball struck Howard in the neck. He was taken to the police station, and attended by Drs. Thompson and Lyons. The ball struck him about in the middle of the throat and passed downward into the lungs. The spinal column is affected, as the left leg was paralyzed soon after the shooting.

"Mrs. Howard was at the police station this morning, and she says that her husband would be insane two or three days when he came out of a fit, and that she had stayed with him many nights when no man could be found brave enough to remain with him. She said that he was in the habit of relating blood curdling adventures in the West till she requested him to cease relating such disagreeable narratives.

"From the statements made to his physicians there can be no doubt that Howard was laboring under a hallucination at the time he attacked Officer Connor. The latter did not know Mr. Howard and naturally supposed that a man, desperate enough to attack a policeman in uniform and attempt to rob him of his watch was a desperate character.

"Howard had not lived with his family for several months (one year, according to Mrs. Howard). Mrs. Howard said she had great control over him when he was bereft of reason and could manage him when men failed to control him.

"Mr. Howard was at the Fitchburg railroad car inspector's shop at about midnight, and his strange behavior was noticed by the men, who notified the police. His physicians have little hope of his recovery."

Photograph by Jack Reneau.

The Howard family plot is located in a cemetery on a hill overlooking Hinsdale, New Hampshire.

Photograph by Jack Reneau.

George's body was laid to rest a few days after he was shot in the neck by a police officer as George walked through a railroad yard in Fitchburg, Massachusetts.

George spoke briefly to his wife and daughters as he lay in the almshouse waiting to die. He told the doctors and his wife that he only asked the time of day of Officer Connor and did not know the man was a police officer. According to George, Officer Connor made a rude remark to Howard when asked the time, and Howard hit Officer Connor in anger. At the trial of Connor in February of 1887, physicians and Mrs. Howard testified about George's comments. The complete testimony of the trial was recorded in the *Fitchburg Sentinel*. Copies of the newspaper, which are no longer published, were found in the Fitchburg library. The hole in his neck and the bullet in his lungs made talking very difficult and painful. He could only whisper to his wife and children as he bled to death. He clung to life until Friday, January 21, when he died at 11:45 a.m. His wife and daughters were there until the end. Grace, six at the time, remembers the blood trickling from his neck and the paleness of his cheeks. He was only able to give a faint smile when he recognized his children, and he looked tortured. Grace's strongest living recollection of her father was when he lay on his deathbed, gasping for breath.

An autopsy was conducted January 22, by Medical Examiner Miller. He determined that the bullet had entered the throat in front, in the median line, passed through the larynx and esophagus, with a tendency slightly to the left and downward. There was an opening into the pleural (lung) cavity, and the ball penetrated the spinal column, without touching the spinal cord, between the first and second dorsal vertebrae, splintering the second rib behind.

From this point, the ball passed through the muscles to a point in the center of the shoulder blade, where it was found beneath the skin and subcutaneous fat. The food he had taken since he was shot passed, for the most part, into the pleural cavity. The left lung was collapsed, and the injuries were fatal. The entire autopsy was published in the *Fitchburg Sentinel* on January 23, 1887.

The body was taken to Hinsdale by train for burial and was buried on Sunday, January 23, in view of his mother, wife, daughters and remaining siblings Amy, Melissa, Philena, Seymour, Lucius, Hannah, Henry, Ellen, and Auburn. Martha Howard did not receive any compensation for his death even though the police officer was convicted of murder and fired from his job. After the burial, a family friend, F. W. Brazier, wrote a letter to the newspaper asking townspeople to make contributions to the family to cover living expenses. There is no record of how many donations (if any at all) were received, but Grace says that life was financially bleak after his death. Martha Howard did not remarry until August 28, 1897, and worked as a laundress and tailor in Fitchburg and Shirley. Grace Howard said that as a teenager her mother remarried a gentle man, Almond R. Hopkins, and life for Martha and her two girls improved.

Martha filed for a widow's pension in 1931, following the death of Almond on October 23, 1918. She was not aware that she was eligible for George's pension until 1931 when relatives told her about the process.

To receive a pension of $30 per month commencing February 10, 1931, Martha was required to submit legal proof of marriage to George and Almond. Her efforts to receive $30 per month from George's pension fund provided many of the legal documents that detail George's life. The entire pension file submitted by Martha in 1931 remains in the National

Archives. Her oldest daughter, Bessie May, submitted a statement to testify that her mother was legally married to both men.

Unfortunately for Martha, she died in 1935, so she did not receive the meager pension for very long, and could have received it after her husband's death if she had only known to apply.

In a short span of 36 years, George S. Howard had witnessed the horrors of the American Civil War as a youthful drummer boy, experienced the excruciating pain of one of the most serious train accidents of the 19th century, and witnessed the destruction of the Native American way of life in the Western Plains as a cavalry scout. He had hunted grizzly, deer, antelope, and elk as far north as the Yellowstone Basin and fished for three-pound trout in most of the rivers and streams of Wyoming, Montana, South Dakota, and Nebraska. He felt himself going insane, and, when he died, he witnessed the suffering of his family as they looked into his tormented eyes as he drew his last breath in a poorhouse.

For five of those 36 years we can peek into his mind and experience his innermost thoughts as he copes with the hardships and new experiences of Western life. He slept with his diary, sometimes using it as a pillow to protect his head from the frosty Montana and Wyoming ground. He curled by a crackling campfire on campaigns through the Black Hills of Dakota writing poetry about lost loves and battles. He carried his diary in the sidesaddle pack as he fought in the battles of Powder River, Rosebud, and Slim Buttes.

Girlfriends and army buddies doodled messages in the margins of his book, and friends had poems dedicated to them. Girlfriends and George himself pasted bits of stationery on pages of the diary to recall letters he received from New England. Important dates in George's life were written beside favorite poems and diary entries, and girlfriends wrote comments about poems and entries.

George knew Red Cloud, Big Rib, Spotted Tail, Old Friday, Old Crow, Red Dog, Redface, Warp Nose, Dull Knife, Little Bear, Sitting Bull, Man-Afraid-of-his-Horse, Bad Face, Crazy Horse, Sly Fox, and Raven Wing. His daughter said he recognized the Indians as they stood ready for battle and exchanged medicine cures with favorite Indian hunters. She said he told hair-raising tales of adventure and death to anyone who would listen.

George S. Howard's spirit did not die, only his body. I feel his ghost looking over my shoulder, as you will when you read his poetry and prose in the second half of this book.

The date of this photograph of George S. Howard is unknown.

Chapter Three

Scenes, Incidents and Sketches of Life in the Far West

The title of this chapter is the title for George's prose section of the diary that was written by him in 1876 and 1877 after he experienced the adventure of the West as a cavalry scout, hunter, and fisherman. His travels around Wyoming Territory, Montana Territory, Dakota Territory, and Nebraska during that time period were recorded in a smaller version of his diary, so he could carry it in his pocket, according to his daughter.

After returning from the Big Horn and Sioux Expeditions, his daughter said he copied his entries into the larger ledger book that contained his poems and other prose. He copied the 1876 campaign prose while stationed at Fort Sanders, Wyoming, from January to May of 1877, and in New Hampshire after returning home from his five-year enlistment.

The poetry and prose were transcribed by me from George's 9- by 13-inch ledger book, one word at a time. Exact punctuation, capitalization, grammar, and spelling used by George is reproduced as it is still seen in the original diary. Comments in italics were written by me to explain entries in the diary. The actual page numbers of a diary entry are to the left of the text in parentheses. To fully understand the context of the diary prose and poetry, read the first four chapters of this book that describe his life and my efforts to understand his times.

Tragically, Grace Howard wrote over the daily entries with a black ink pen as the original ink began to fade, so translation was more difficult. To properly transcribe the diary, each page was held up to a strong light and examined through a magnifying glass. Books and newspaper articles helped to piece together the details of the diary.

(PAGE 220)

It was a pleasant sunny Morn about the 20th of October 1872 that I left Springfield, Mass. for the purpose of travelling for a few years among new scenes and strange faces. Owing to affliction in New England I wished to leave it for awhile, little dreaming that no where else on earth I should find the sympathizing friends I was going to leave behind Me in the home of my childhood.

Yet such is our life always verifying the old saying that "Experience is a hard school but one in which many valuable lessons are taught."

Scenes, Incidents and Sketches of Life in the Far West

It was a pleasant sunny Morn about the 20th of Oct, 1872 that I left Spring field Mass for the purpose of travelling for a few years among new scenes and strange faces owing to affliction in New England I wished to leave it for a while little dreaming that no where else on earth I should find the sympathizing friends I was going to leave behind me in the Home of my childhood. Yet such is our life always verifying the old saying that "Experience is a hard school but one in which many valuable lessons are taught" A pleasant afternoons ride took me over to Albany at which place I stopped a week or more when one splendid night I stepped aboard the steamer Drew of the night line and started down the river and to those of you who have never travelled that beautiful river I would recommend you to do so if chance ever offers. You get to Sing Sing about daylight in the summer and from there to New York the view is as fine as you will see in any settled portion of the United States. Although I have since seen finer Natural prospects yet I never have seen any thing that looked so bright and fresh showing how well through civilization could make the Earth to teem with peace and plenty, as did this Autumn prospect on the lower Hudson After reaching New York how different the smoky hurrying city it seems but little like the quiet and contentment I had just left behind yet this is the center of the Universe to Americans and as you travel through its multitude of streets you wonder how all these people in so little space lin

The first page of George S. Howard's diary that describes his trip to Wyoming Territory in October of 1872. George's daughter Grace wrote over this page entry with a dark pen because the original blue ink began to fade. Several pages in the diary were written over by Grace, making exact translations more difficult.

A pleasant afternoons ride took me over to Albany *[New York]*, at which place I stopped a week or more. When one splendid night I stepped aboard the steamer Drew of the night line and started down the river *[Hudson River]*. And, to those of you who have never travelled that beautiful river I would recommend you do so if chance ever offers.

You get to Sing Sing about daylight in the summer, and from there to New York *[City]* the view is as fine as you will see in any settled part of the United States. Although I have since seen finer Natural prospects, yet I never have seen any thing that looked so bright and fresh, showing how we, through civilization could make the Earth to teem with peace and plenty as did this autumn prospect on the Lower Hudson.

After reaching New York, how different the smoky hurrying city. It seems but little like the quiet and contentment I had just left behind. Yet this is the center of the Universe to Americans, and as you travel through its multitude of streets you wonder how all these people live in so little space.

(PAGE 221)

But that is some thing one half of New York does not know of the other half—not to give any extended description of the City but to those who have never been there I would recommend them to some fine bright morning go down in to the Battery and there spend an hour. See the ships coming in and going out.

The little steam tugs plying their trade busy as bees before you on the waters of the bay and rivers—you see the commerce of most nearly all Nations. There can be seen the Flags of 11 or 12 Nationalitys of any morning but the Sun will grow higher and you will want to see many other places and things. so take the route up East River and see the big bridge and see what man can do—from there go up the hill by some of the numerous streets and see the Post Office. Just above the City hall is inclosed in a little park or common. it was here that I saw the body of H. Greeley *[Newspaper publisher Horace Greeley, who reportedly said, "Go West Young Man, Go West"]* lying in state, and many a famed name has this little building held, names dear to all ages and all climes.

From here take the cars to Central Park and there you have a view like that on the Hudson only not so stupendous in its appointments, but more of the works of man. I had not stopped here long 'ere that great man Horace Greeley slept the sleep that knows no waking. And to see the respect shown him. you should have seen the procession that followed his corpse to the last resting place. Standing on the summit of Broadway just above the City Hall as far as the eye could see naught but mourners paying the last sad tribute to the illustrous dead but this was soon to be followed by the disastrous fire in the Fifth Avenue Hotel where so many women lost their lives, that was a heart rending time for the poor mothers who had girls working there, but concluding that it would not suit me for a residence.

Next morning took the coach

(PAGE 222)

for the land of the Buffalo and the deer passing the justly celebrated Horse shoe bend in the Mountains on a clear moon light night with the earth covered with snow. and it is a fine sight showing how man has triumphed over nature in her strongholds. Here you pass Among these

This sketch of Cheyenne, Wyoming, in 1876 includes the Inter-Ocean Hotel to the right. According to Crofutt's Trans-Continental Tourist's Guide *Cheyenne grew from one house in 1867 to 6,000 inhabitants in 1877 with a lively exchange of business activity.*

A portion of Cheyenne, Wyoming, as it appeared in 1876. In 1877, Cheyenne boasted a $40,000 courthouse and the $70,000 Inter-Ocean Hotel, plus an opera house and several schools and churches. Three daily newspapers were published.

mountains you see age old locomotives, dirty and disagreeable looking, but of great value here. Never the less, taking what is known as the Pan Handle Route, you are whirled through tunnels and over bridges along beside of the old unused canal for many miles passing the smoking City of Pittsburg in the night 'till finally you stop at Columbus *[Ohio]* for an hour or two and take a walk through the principal streets. the first thing a stranger will notice is the extreme width of the streets and the prosperous healthy look of the City.

But it is not far enough West and the train finds me whirling along through Indianapolis *[Indiana]* and across the southern part of Illinois through a sparsely settled country to St. Louis at which place there was a large rail road bridge. Watching at that time one peculiarity of the river here at this season of the year, it is nearly covered with crows feeding upon the offal from the large Slaughtering establishments located here. I only stopped here over Sunday, my last sabbath almost in civilization for several years.

Tuesday morning I took the train over the Mo. *[Missouri River]*, through Jefferson *[Jefferson City, Missouri]* and on to Kansas City. then north to Council Bluffs. across the River to Omaha. then over the U.P.R.R. *[Union Pacific Railroad]* to Cheyenne *[Wyoming]*. The country from Omaha to Cheyenne is the most like that in Conn. *[Connecticut]* as the soil. I should say the great wants of the West are wood and water, there being no trees scarcely from Omaha to Cheyenne.

(PAGE 223)

And, good water is not overly plenty any where from Cheyenne. I travelled from there up to Fort Laramie, a Post having been in existence some 29 or 30 years. here you get into a very desert, nothing growing there but Prickly Pears, Rattlesnakes, and Ants. There is about the same amount of game here as there is on the R.R. *[railroad]*: a few antelope, Black and White Tail Deer, sometimes Elk but no Buffalo up here, although they are found on Rivers further north. there are some bear in the black Hills, both Grizzly, Black and Cinnamon but They are not very plenty.

I remember in South Park of seeing six (6) Grizzly Bear together. We had killed 7 Deer that day and had loaded them onto two horses, and the time it took to cut the pack thongs and "git," as we say out there, was short and none too soon either for the bear were there before we were rifle shot away. You may think it was cowardly not to have attacked them, but having been on the Plains before, we both knew better than to attack 6 Grizzlys, for two men had better hesitate about attacking one some times, for they are bad customers to make the best of it. for a Grizzly weighing 12 to 15 hundred is on the fight you can bet. But, there was no necessity for our attacking them for game was plenty, and at night we counted 5 more Deer and 1 mountain sheep. making but a poor day's work for the South Park. for it is as good hunting ground as the Plains can boast, or was at that time. It lies to the South of the U.P.R.R. from Laramie City for 200 miles nearly and it is 80 or 100 miles wide.

(PAGE 224)

But, the most of my hunting was done north of the Rail Road making my headquarters at Fort Laramie or near there at Cunge Ranche or at Fort Fetterman 95 miles North. I have killed many a deer, Antelope, and Bear on the Horseshoe, the Chug, the Cottonwood, the

Photograph by John Reneau.

Fort Laramie today includes eleven buildings built in the 1800s that have been restored. Shown is Lt. Col. Andrew Burt's home (c. 1884), the Post Trader's Store (1849), and the cavalry barracks (1874). Old Army records at the National Archives record that these barracks were constructed by men stationed at the fort in the early 1870s.

Photograph by John Reneau.

The Old Army Bridge or the Fort Laramie Bridge was completed in 1875 by soldiers from Fort Laramie to span the turbulent North Platte River. The bridge became a vital link to the gold fields of the Black Hills and other military posts. This bridge was constructed by men stationed at the fort in 1875.

Elkhorn at Le Bounty, Wagon Hound, and on the Rawhide and Loco Coke or Running Water. At this time, there was a sawmill at or near Laramie Peak where I occasionally stopped nights. From there to the head waters of the Horse shoe was ten miles, so I could go there in a day and it was a great place for game. The largest herd of Elk I ever saw was at Moss agate hill. it contained about 700 I think. but the best of the hunting grounds north of the R.R. *[railroad]* was Laramie Plains reaching from Cheyenne to Laramie City, just north of the R.R. At the time it fairly teemed with deer of all kinds.

Some times in my hunts I saw trails of Indians and then I had to be careful for I did not wish for any trouble though no 10 Sioux will trouble 2 hunters without they can get the drop on them. Our dogs or ponies would smell them more than Rifle shot off.

I suppose you would arrest me for cruelty to animals. Could you see me chasing Elk on a pony who would not weigh more than six hundred and myself and outfit weighing 250 at least? But small as Bill was he could out run Elk if they were surprised, for then they take a lope that cannot take them along very fast. But when they came down to the pace, good bye Elk, for no horse or pony can keep up them they will go a mile in less than 2 minutes, and that is fast over sage brush and bluffs!

Laramie

(PAGE 225)

This place was once almost the best known of the Frontier Posts. Here the Overland Trail branched off to Colorado, to Montana, and California. Here in Summer time might be seen thousands of emigrants traveling toward the setting sun to find the Gold hidden in the Rivers and darkening caves of the Far West. That land then looks to people in the States almost like that "born from which no traveller e'er returns."

Here too could be seen plenty of Red men: Ogletatas, Cheyennes, Arapahoes, Brule Sioux of all colors and bands. Here can sometimes be seen now Red Cloud, Spotted Tail, Old Friday, Old Crow *[Crow King]*, Big Rib, Red Dog, Redface, Warp Nose, Dull Knife, Little Bear, Sitting bull, Man afraid of his horse and others who had not dare come near the White man like Bad Face and Crazy Horse of the Minnieconjous, the tribe that committed the depredations in '73 and '74. They are no tribe exactly but outlaws from all tribes of the Sioux Nation, also halfbreeds from the settled portion of the territories and with them are the two Reshaws well known around Laramie for their depredations.

I soon from my knowledge of the Country used to accompany the Cavalry in their raids, for any trail that I had once seen I could follow and all the isolated Buttes had marks on them that I never forgot. For there you must know every morning just where you are or you will soon get lost, for the country looks the same from almost any stand point.

In August of '72, I was guiding 2 Companies of Cavalry under the command of Capt. Egan *[Capt. James Egan]* and we had followed the trail of the Reds for 100 miles at least, when one morning I told him where the Indians were for I found them in the night. But such is the great sagacity of

Spotted Tail, a chief of the Brule Sioux, defied the orders of white generals and rose up to defend his lands from miners, settlers, and soldiers. He was born in 1833 near Fort Laramie and was killed by Crow Dog near the Rosebud Agency, Dakota Territories, in 1881. He is mentioned in George S. Howard's diary.

(PAGE 226)

Army Officers that no citizen can tell them anything, and considering his judgement better than mine, he rode on to the Bluff just above them and gave them time to get 2 miles start before we got across the creek to where we could chase them. But after a hard run of 12 miles we captured 22 ponies and mules, some guns of different kinds, their bows and arrows. So they just got away with their lives and that was nearly all.

The next time I was sent there, how different. In the afternoon of February 11th '74, the Post was alive with rumors that a Lieut. of Infantry *[Lt. Levi Herbert Robinson of the 14th Infantry]* and a Corporal of Cavalry *[Corp. James Coleman of Company K, 2nd Cavalry]* had been killed by some fifty Indians near where we took the Ponies from the Indians in August. I was sent out on the melancholy duty of trying to find their bodies if possible. And, it was a sad trip for us all before we got through, for we all had some hope that it was not so. But it was alas! too true. We left the Post at 11 o'clock at night, rode till morning. Took hasty breakfast & in the saddle again for the Canyon at 11 that forenoon. We got skirmishers out and I began to look over the Ravine to find a trace, for ponies will show where they go and all the Redman's cunning cannot prevent it. I found the trail in half mile and started on it but we kept the skirmishers out, not knowing but what they might have turned back or killed some Indians. But I found the first sign of the bloody fray, which was the body of the Corporal shot first through the head which was his mistake wound.

(PAGE 227)

A little further on we found the body of the Lieut., but where shot first was hard to say. He lay in a little Ravine out from the main Canyon, with his hands clenched as though in agony when death came. He was shot with bullets in the right cheek twice, through the right leg once,. thumb of left hand was shot off. He wore a knit jacket and this was put together and an arrow driven through it. 2 other arrows stuck up in his breast, and a fourth had been shot directly through his breast and broken off. Arrows had cut his forehead and they were not mutilated except shots of balls and that of arrows.

The Lieut. had 13 wounds but all were in front or face; the Corporal had 11 and all in back. It showed the Indian way of discriminating Bravery and Cowardice, for the Corporal had not pulled off his gloves, but the Lieut. had apparently used his revolver but to what extent I could not say. He had a watch in his pocket which was not disturbed, showing that plunder was not their object.

But the melancholy duty was not over and we took the bodies and started for the Post, a sad silent party. Had we but met the Reds that day they would of got something unusual, that was justice, yet, still this is, "Lo, the Poor Indian." *[Mr. Lo was the standard Army expression for Indians, singular and plural. The expression originated from a poem, "Essay on Man."]*

All around here at Laramie we see the worst of the warfare, from the arrival of the White man 'till now. Near the Peak *[Laramie Peak]* is a stockade where 14 of the 11th Ohio Volunteer Company were seiged nine days 'till help came. All over this Country the bones of the 11th lie bleaching beside hundreds of graves that no man knows of.

This old trail is lined with Ruined Ranches and graves. Here many sleep who started for the country of gold and died. Here many

(PAGE 228)

sleep who were looked for and longed for years without number. Where the tomahawk and scalping knife have done their work for years and still the war goes on. Still the general have them escorted on to their reservations very kindly and always give them a good visit as did Capt. Egan in August '73.

I do not consider myself qualified to say how the tribes of Indians that are left of the once great Nation of Aborigines should be treated but the present policy is "played out." The land near Fort Laramie is not worth reclaiming. Yet we have started to subdue the Indians and let it be done. We all thought the Modoc fearful bad but then prior to the murder of Gen. Canby they were not half so bad as the Brule Sioux of Wyoming. *[Brig. Gen. E. R. S. Canby was killed by the Modoc Indians in the Lava Beds of California during the Modoc Campaign, April 11 to 20, 1873. The campaign lasted from November 29, 1872, to June 1, 1873.]*

Although the old chiefs are afraid yet they cannot control the young braves and so it still goes on this fearful Indian war or series of murders. It was here that myself and comrades riding out together one afternoon trying to get some game were jumped by 18 who tried to procure a couple of scalps but that was one of the times they failed for we were passing through a canyon when ahead I saw something move. And, creeping up close in spite of the fear of my pony, I saw the Indians and making the sign to all that they were Reds and so to many for us we crept back but they discovered it and in less time than it takes to tell it they were after us, but it was to their sorrow for in the 11 miles they chased us they lost 5 of their men and another one wounded so they thought we were not worth the powder and let us slide. Many a Sioux has bit the dust before the rifles of myself and Pard's. Yet still the Government says it is such as us that make the trouble

(PAGE 229)

on the border, and I never did shoot an Indian except in self-defense.

After two months after this happened, I killed one of the largest Panthers on the border, at least I never heard of a larger one. While riding along the trail one day I saw something leaping through the snow some 6 hundred yards off. And he was coming nearer to me. I saw it was a very large panther. And up with my rifle and let him have it. I broke his left shoulder and with a bite at the wound he came at me as fast as 2 feet of snow would permit, and I shot again with my rifle but I did not stop him, and pulling out my revolver and quieting my horse, I was ready for the struggle and as he got within 20 yards I let him have it and fired. He died within 16 feet of me and measured 11 ft. 7 in. from tip to tip and was shot in 6 places, one shot going in one ear and lodging in the brain.

(PAGE 230)

The Summer Campaign of 1876

The following entries in George's diary detail his day-to-day activity during the summer campaign of 1876, a campaign that included many battles with the Sioux and Cheyenne Nations. George was appointed to hunt meat and fish for his company. This detailed section occurs after the poem section of the book. The actual page numbers of where the entries are located

Dr. Valentine T. McGillycuddy, one of several doctors on the summer campaign of 1876, beside his pine bough hut just after the Horsemeat or Starvation March of September 1876 in the Dakota Territories.

are in parentheses. The Battle of Powder River George refers to in his first entry is also described in poetry form on pages 193 to 200 in the diary.

His entries were compared to the monthly reports filed by commanding officers for his company and with the daily diaries of officers who were on the same campaigns. The summer reports by the commanding officers are missing from the regimental files in the National Archives, so diaries of officers and enlisted men like George S. Howard were the most comprehensive details available in 1876.

Apr 18th   As I kept no record of the 1st Trip this Spring I shall have to write it from memory. We have been on one of the most severe trips I have heard of. It was one continual round of Snow storms and when it was not snowing it was very cold. We made two night marches, one from Crazy Woman Fork to Clear Creek the other from the head of Mizpah River to the Powder River. Each was of thirty-five miles, or more. The one from the Mizpah River being the night of Mar 16th the Night before the Crazy Horse fight of Mar 17th. This was a fight lasting Five hours in which we lost 4 killed and 7 wounded. Their loss was 104 Lodges burned and 700 Ponies captured by Our Troops. During the Trip we had 4 night alarms and on Mar 17th we alarmed them. We travelled with Pack Mules from the 7th until the 22nd. Making some 340 miles. From the Crazy Woman Fork to Tongue River down Tongue to a creek running up toward the Mizpah up this to the Mizpah. Thence over to the Powder and up the Powder to Old Fort Reno. One herder was shot and the Beef stolen the 2nd night out from Fetterman. we at the time camping on the South Cheyenne.

[Reporter Robert E. Strahorn's complete accounting of the Battle of Powder River is found in the Library of Congress with the microfilmed copies of the Rocky Mountain Tribune (News) *dated April 4, 1876. He marched with the soldiers during the campaign and gave a personal impression of the "most severe trip" as only a professional journalist can do. He also listed a soldier from Company E, 2nd Cavalry, who may have been the man George Howard rescued named Corp. John Lang who was shot through the right ankle. George composes several poems about the Battle of Powder River and only mentions the Battle of the Rosebud and Slim Buttes which indicates how much the Powder River battle meant to him.]*

May 19th   Left Fort D.A. Russell at 1 o'clock P.M. marched to Pole Creek. The road today was over sand Hills and through bottoms or hollows suitable for grazing. A Fine day. 15 miles.

[Fort D. A. Russell was renamed Warren Air Force Base near Cheyenne, Wyoming, to honor Civil War hero and first Wyoming state governor, Francis E. Warren, in 1930. The fort was established on July 21, 1867, three miles west of Cheyenne on the north bank of Crow Creek to protect Union Pacific Railroad crews and white settlers of the new Frontier city. Soldiers considered it one of the most beautiful of the Western posts. Its location on the railroad line and near the South Platte River made it an immediate and important supply depot for Western communities and forts. Col. Christopher C. Augur, 12th Infantry, selected the fort's site and

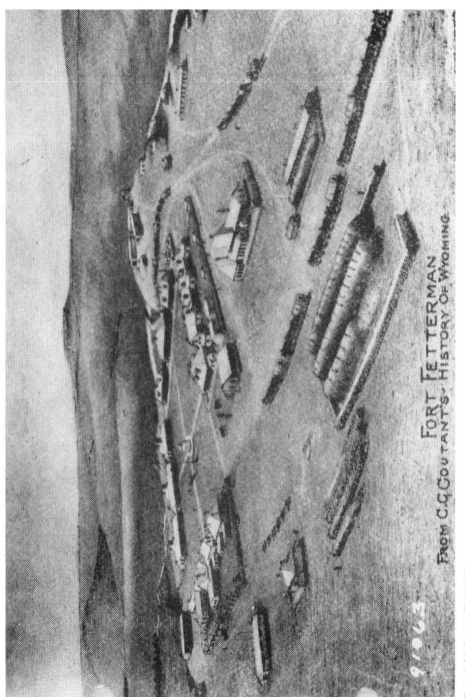

FORT FETTERMAN

FROM C.G.COUTANTS- HISTORY OF WYOMING.

Photograph of sketch courtesy of National Archives.

Counted as a hardship tour of duty by Army troops, Fort Fetterman was established in July of 1867 as the last post on the Indian border. George stayed at the fort while waiting for further orders in February of 1876 before the Big Horn Expedition. This 1870 sketch shows the cluster of plank and adobe buildings and parade ground.

Col. John D. Stevenson, 30th Infantry, oversaw the development of the site. Today a museum and tour are open to the public.]

May 20th   Left Pole Creek at 5:30 A.M. and marched to Bear Springs. The road was over a succession of high table lands. Road hard and good. Weather fair and calm.

May 21st   Left Camp at Bear Springs at 6:15 A.M. Marched to Kelly's Ranch on the Chugwater Creek Road. Lay over a succession of sand hills and through ravines. Watered. Then Mounted and marched to Huntoons Ranche. The Road going down the Creek bottom past Chimney Rock of the Laramie Trail. Weather fair. 12 miles. Wind blew. Cloudy. Rain. Good Road, nearly level. Passed 8 Ranches on the

(Page 231)
Creek today. This is one of the finest bottoms in the Western Country. Very disagreeable tonight.

May 22nd Lay over on ac'ct of the Storm. Camp about 1 mile below Huntoon's Ranche. It rained all day and got very muddy and disagreable. Rain.

May 23rd Left Camp at 5:20 A.M. marched to Fort Laramie. The Road was over a series of sand hills and along the foot of Clay-Bluffs. Road good despite the excessive rain the soil being of a gravelly character the rain could not affect it much. Fort Laramie is one of the finest Posts to soldier at on the Plains it has accommodations for 6 Co's of Infantry and 2 of Cavalry. It is 95 miles from Cheyenne. It is located on a low bluff. 1-1/2 miles from the mouth of the Laramie River. the soil in the neighborhood of the Post is poor, being gravel mostly and grows only prickly pears, Rattlesnakes and Prairie Dogs. Cloudy. Fair. 28 miles.

May 24th Left Ft. Laramie at 6:15 A.M. crossed the North Platte River just above the mouth of the Laramie. Took the trail (for it is little more here) on the North side of the River. Marched all day over gravelly bluffs and through the River bottom. A great deal of Conglomerate rock here showing where the gravel has petrified. Some Sandstone here. Camped tonight on the Platte about 6 miles below Bulls Bend in one of the finest bottoms on the River. Two Graves here. One Narcissia Givens 1834. The other, Ripley 1862. Cloudy. Cool. 28 miles.

May 25th Left Camp at 5:25 this A.M. Made a detour over the Bluffs crossing one Creek. Came back to the River near Bridgers Ferry Road. Today over a fine country but devoid of wood and water with the exception of Creek above noticed. Cloudy A.M. Fair P.M. 30 miles.

May 26th   Left Camp this A.M. at 6:30. Marched in the Platte Valley past the renowned Bridger Ferry. Through a very fine grazing country today. Camped tonight on the River. Saw today 9 White Tail and a few Antelope. Fair, hot and dusty. 23 miles.

May 27th   Left Camp this A.M. at 5:40. Marched to Fort Fetterman arrived at 11:15. Camped opposite the Post on the North side of the Platte River. The Road today lay through the bottom and up on some bluffs. A part of the celebrated bad lands. C and G of the Third left for a Scout toward

(Page 232)
the headwaters of the Powder River. Lots of rabbits and butterflies to catch. 12 miles.

May 28th   Laid in Camp today. On Guard. Here ready for the Expedition A, B, C, D, E, F, G, I, M, L of the 3rd Cavalry. A, B, D, E, I and K Second Cavalry. And Six Co's of the 9th and 4th Infantry. Fair.

May 29th   Left Ft. Fetterman today at 2:30 P.M. Marched to Sage Creek. Road very good. 16 miles.

May 30th   Left Camp on Sage Creek this A.M. at 7:15. Marched over a white clay country for 15 miles. Watered at Brown's Springs. Then went on to the South Fork of Cheyenne River where our first skirmish occurred on the other Expedition. Wind blowing. 20 miles.

May 31st   Left Camp on So. Fork Cheyenne at 7 A.M. Marched over the ridges past Stinking Water (18 miles) to the No. Fork Cheyenne. Good grazing Country, if the Indians should be driven away. Wood Cottonwood and only on the Borders of the Streams. Cold, windy, cloudy. 23 miles.

June 1st   Left Camp on No. F. Cheyenne at 6:45. Marched on top of Ridges mostly today. Camped at Antelope Springs near Dry Fork [of the] Powder River. Poor Water. Found board saying a party of Miners under Capt. St. John left here May 27th for Deadwood, Black Hills, D.T. had no trouble with Indians coming from Montana here. 24 miles. Snow squalls all day.

June 2nd   Left Camp at Antelope Springs at 7:05 A.M. Marched down Dry Fork, Powder River 12 miles then over the Ridge to the Powder, striking the River opposite the Ruins of Fort Reno, abandoned in '68. Crossed the River and camped in the Bottom below Reno Road good plenty of Cottonwood on the banks of the River. No trouble with Indians yet. 18 miles. Cold, cloudy.

"Lay over in Camp on Tongue River...The Indians gave us a little performance this evening. Some 50 or 60 on the Bluffs on the other side of the River in hopes to draw out a small party to follow them," said George S. Howard on June 8 and 9, 1876. Charles G. Stanley drew this event for Frank Leslie's Illustrated Newspaper.

[Fort Reno was established on August 14, 1865, on a bluff rising 50-feet above the left bank of the Powder River about 22 miles from present-day Kaycee. Brig. Gen. Patrick E. Connor established the fort to protect miners and settlers who traveled the Bozeman Trail. He called it by his name until the name officially changed to Fort Reno in honor of Civil War hero Maj. Jesse L. Reno who died in the Battle of South Mountain in 1862. The fort was abandoned on August 18, 1868, when white generals signed the Fort Laramie Treaty with the Sioux chiefs in April of that year. Indians immediately burned the fort and white settlers established Cantonment Reno near the site in 1876 during the Big Horn Expedition. The second site was eventually called Fort McKinney or McKinney Depot in honor of Lt. John A. McKinney, 4th Infantry, who was killed by Indians in 1876. The depot was eventually moved near the present-day city of Buffalo. Robert W. Frazer in his book, Forts of the West, *gives a clear description of the various Western forts as do records found in the National Archives from military officers.]*

June 3rd   Left Camp at Fort Reno at 6:30 A.M. Marched over Ridges to Crazy Woman Fork of Powder River. The country very good for grazing, yet no wood, only on the streams. 32 miles. Fine weather.

June 4th   Saw 6 Indians last night. Left Camp this morning at 6:30. Marched to Clear Creek Road over a succession of Ridges and through Gulches crossing another Dry Fork of Powder River. Road good, no wood only on the Streams. 2 Watering places on the road. 21 miles. Fine, warm.

June 5th   Left Camp on Clear Fork at 7:30. Marched to Old Fort Phil Kearney *[The correct spelling is "Kearny."]* Passed plenty of Water on the Road. Road Good. Not much wood. Storm brewing.

(PAGE 233)
This trail is just East of the Big Horn Mts. Passed Lake De Smet, a fine little lake some 2 miles in length by 1/2 mile in width. *[Lake De Smet exists today.]* 20 miles. Fine, warm.

[The remnants of Fort Kearny at the foot of Big Horn (Bighorn) Mountains are open today to the public during spring and summer months. The Wyoming State Museum says that the fort was established in July of 1866 between the confluence of Big and Little Piney Creeks near the present-day towns of Story and Buffalo to protect settlers who traveled the Bozeman Trail. Lake De Smet is between these two present-day towns. The fort was named for Civil War hero Maj. Gen. Philip Kearny, who was killed at the Battle of Chantilly, Virginia, in 1862. The fort was abandoned in 1868 and burned by the Sioux after the Fort Laramie Treaty of April 29, 1868, was signed. The Sioux and Cheyenne were very dissatisfied with the Laramie agreement because it did not protect their sacred hunting grounds in the Black Hills from miners and settlers.]

This illustration from Frank Leslie's Illustrated Newspaper shows Gen. George Crook's army crossing the west fork of Goose Creek on June 16, 1876. George S. Howard wrote, "On June 16, we left camp this A.M. at 5 o'clock. Marched down Goose Creek 5 miles to its junction with Tongue River then down the North side of the River 12 miles to a small creek, name unknown . . ."

June 6th   Left Camp at Old Fort Phil Kearney at 7:30 A.M. Marched past the scene of the Massacre of November 28, 1867 over Ridges to a Creek, name unknown. *[Creek that George did not know may have been Little Goose Creek outside of present-day Banner.]* Down the Creek until we made 17 miles. The Road poor from long disuse. The Country was the finest I ever have seen for Stock. Water good. Wood rather scarce. Cottonwood mostly. It was very hot until near night when a Thunder shower cooled it off some. 19 miles. Fine, thunder shower.

June 7th   Came on down Prairie Dog Creek today. Road good. Rained in the forenoon but cleared up in the P.M. Good Water and Wood in plenty. Camped tonight on Tongue River a beautiful stream, beautifully fringed with large Cottonwood groves. 14 miles.

June 8th   Lay over in Camp on Tongue River. I Company 2nd, captured one Pony and killed 2 Buffalo. Buried a man of B Company 3rd Cav. here named Tiernay. *[Private Andrew Tierney was listed on the monthly U.S. Army report as dead.]*

June 9   Lay Over in Camp. Very disagreeable day. The Indians gave us a little performance this evening. Some 50 or 60 came on the Bluffs on the other side of the River in hopes to draw out a small party to follow them. They were finally driven away by 4 Co's of the 3rd Cav. Some spent bullets came over near my tent but no one was hurt. one mule and one horse was shot. Showery.

[The horse shot and killed was a white mare belonging to Major Burt, according to Lt. John G. Bourke, who wrote a detailed diary of his 15-year adventures with Gen. George Crook including the summer campaign of 1876. Bourke's writings were from the perspective of an officer. George's diary was from the perspective of an enlisted man and ground soldier. Bourke said the horse shot was one of the troop's favorites for horse racing to pass away the endless camp hours which may explain why George made mention in his diary of the horse's death. A reporter for the New York Herald, *Reuben Briggs Davenport, had his detailed account of the skirmish published in the newspaper on June 16, 1876. This newspaper article was found in the Library of Congress. This battle is referred to by historians as a skirmish at Tongue River Heights that took place about 26 miles northwest of present-day Sheridan, Wyoming, near Columbus Peak.]*

June 10th   Laid in Camp. Showers almost every afternoon. Weather pretty good.

June 11th   Left Camp at 8 A.M. Took the back trail for about 7 miles, then crossed over the Goose Creek. Road today good, the Country the prettiest I have seen on the Plains. Camp tonight one of the finest we have ever camped at. 11 miles. Fair, Showers.

[Gen. Crook refers to this camp as Big Goose Creek which was located in present-day Sheridan, Wyoming. Crook and his troops set out at this point to locate Sioux and Cheyenne encampments reported to be along the Little Big Horn River in southern Montana.]

This illustration of the Battle of the Rosebud on June 17, 1876, by Charles G. Stanley, is from Frank Leslie's Illustrated Newspaper. George S. Howard wrote in his diary, "Three months to the day since the Powder River Fight with Crazy Horse's band . . . we saw another Performance (battle)." One week later, Col. George Armstrong Custer and his men met their doom.

June 12th Lay in Camp at the mouth of Goose Creek. Last night was very bad, both wet and cold. I was on Piquet *[guard duty]* and had to lie out in the rain all night. We came near unloading our carbines in favor of a Coyote who desired to inspect our Post. The Country here is very fine, being full of Game: Elk, Deer and Buffalo. "I" Company killed one Brown Bear. There are some Trout in the creeks but they do not bite very well now. Rainy.

(PAGE 234)

June 13th Lay over in Camp. Capt. Wells went fishing and caught 19 Trout, the largest weighing 2 lbs. 11 oz. Pretty good.

June 14 Still Lying on Goose Creek. Company being on Piquet we had Breakfast by the light of the stars. Frank Guiard *[Grouard or Gruard were the common spellings of this scout to Gen. George Crook who led the general and his troops throughout the West during the Big Horn Campaign.]* came in today at 12:45 P.M. with six (6) Indians and one (1) half-breed. 165 Crow Indians came in today in the early evening. We did not know they were friendly until they got quite near and we were some distance from Camp so had to use a little discretion. Gathered up our Horses and got ready for a Fight but at the last we rec'd orders from the Comd'g officer that they were friendly so we did not have the Skirmish after all. 86 Shoshones came in quite late in the evening. Fine weather.

June 15 Lay over and got ready to go out tomorrow for 4 days. The Infantry mounted on Pack Mules and the Rations carried on the Horses. Fine.

[Soldiers were issued hardtack, bacon, coffee, and plus 100 rounds of ammunition for a four-day march as described in J. W. Vaughn's book, With Crook at the Rosebud.*]*

June 16 Left Camp this A.M. at 5 o'clock. Marched down Goose Creek 5 miles to its junction with Tongue River, then down the North side of the River 12 miles to a small creek, name unknown. Followed the creek up for 6 miles then across to the Rosebud 10 miles. The Country was good and covered with Buffalo, the Indian Scouts killing 7 or 8. 33 miles. Friday.

[George was one of 1,325 men assembled for the march which included 1,000 officers and enlisted men of the infantry and cavalry, 176 Crow scouts, 86 Shoshone scouts, 20 packers, and 65 miners according to the regimental rolls at the National Archives. The abundance of buffalo in this area impressed George and several diary writers.]

June 17 Three months today since the Powder River Fight with Crazy Horse's band and we started early this Morning and went down the Rosebud Creek 6 or 7 miles, then halted for a while on account of the Scouts having seen some Indian's hunting Buffalo and soon another Performance began. The Shoshones commenced the Skrimmage or the Sioux commenced on them, the first shot breaking a Shoshone's leg. We were unsaddled at the time and through the inefficiency were nearly an hour saddling up, but then we had a hot fight with some 2,600 well mounted Indians, our Command consisting of 15 Co's of Cav. and 5 of Infantry. The Result as near as I can learn from personal observation are 20 Enlisted Men and 1 Officer, "Capt. Henry of the 3rd Cav." *[Capt. Guy V. Henry]*, Shot through the face, Wounded. 9 Enlisted Men and one Shoshone Scout killed. The bodies were all recovered more or less mangled except one who was so badly cut up that he could not be brought away. One Company not being engaged in the close fighting and having a careful Company Commander had no losses. It is known for

(PAGE 235)

certain we killed 19 Indians and how many more is not known at present. After fighting sometime we charged down the canyon to find the village but the gulch was so favorable for an ambush that we turned and came back so we found nothing of them. Saw the Indians off at the distance of 5 or 6 miles going toward the Little Big Horn River but Ammunition being nearly expended and only two days Rations more we had to give up the pursuit. The Fighting was so poorly conducted that the Enemy came in our rear and stole everything left back where we were when the fight commenced. The soldiers have lost all confidence in General Crook. Fine weather. Saturday.

[A detailed account of this battle is in the book by Neil C. Mangum titled, Battle of the Rosebud: Prelude to the Little Bighorn. *Mangum says that ten men were killed in the battle, including one Indian scout, and 21 soldiers were wounded. Reporter Reuben Briggs Davenport had his personal account of the battle published in the* New York Herald *on July 6, 1876, which can be read and copied in the Library of Congress.]*

June 18   Broke Camp rather late this A.M. Marched up the Rosebud and over the divide onto Canyon Creek. Another disastrous retreat with nothing accomplished. The Country is fine with lots of dead buffalo killed by the Sioux and they then hurrying off to fight us or killed to prevent our party from getting them to eat. The Crow Indians went home tonight. Road good. Poor water in Camp tonight and no wood. Fine. 21 miles.

June 19th   Left Camp on Canyon Creek this A.M. at 6 o'clock and Marched over the Little Panther Mountains and other Ridges. Crossed Tongue River 12 miles from Camp. Wood on Creeks. Good grass. Went into Camp on Goose Creek some 2 miles from Old Camp. Fine. 23 miles.

June 20   Marched up the Creek some 8 miles for the purpose of getting grazing for the Stock. We are in a Country good for game, fine water and plenty of wood. Caught a Trout weighing about 1-1/2 lbs. It made a good supper. Wounded all doing well. 8 miles. Fine and hot.

June 21   The wagon train and Wounded left today for Ft. Fetterman. The Rumor is that they bring more troops and some artillery. The Capt. went Fishing with 7 others and they brought Home 93 Trout weighing from 1/2 to 3 lbs. Shot prairie Hen today. Another good Supper. Very warm.

June 22   Lying over on Goose Creek. Went fishing. Caught 6 Trout weighing 11-1/2 lbs. Shot one Duck. I am so full that I don't think I will ever be hungry again! Warm.

June 23   Lying over. Courier from Ft. Fetterman dispatch is 8 Co's of 5th Cavalry at *[Fort]* Laramie under Lt. Col. Carr [Lt. Col. Eugene A. Carr] coming out here. Signs of Indians today. Gen'l Terry [Brig. Gen. Alfred H. Terry] had fight crossing the Yellowstone about 100 killed on the two sides and about equally divided.

(PAGE 236)

June 24   Moved Camp for grazing. Going up the Creek 4-1/2 miles on Piquet again. Scouts Report large Village of the Enemy to the North. Smoke of several large fires seen towards the north. Thought to be Col. John Gibbon's from Ellis, Montana. 4-1/2 miles. Hot.

[The fires were the campfires of the Sioux and Cheyenne gathering for the Battle of the Little Big Horn that took place June 25 and 26 in which Col. George A. Custer, 12 other officers, and 189 enlisted men were killed.]

June 25   On guard. No news to write. Weather very warm. Everything quiet. Moving the Commissary up from Lower Camp. Hot.

[Jerome A. Greene, Western historian, has reproduced several personal accounts from various newspapers and books in his new book, Battles and Skirmishes of the Great Sioux War, 1876-1877: The Military View. *A fascinating account of the Battle of Little Big Horn is found in Chapter 4 by William "Billy" Jackson, an Indian scout for Custer, who begins his story with Custer's departure from the mouth of Rosebud Creek on June 22, 1876. William died in 1901 on the Blackfoot Reservation in Montana.]*

June 26   Went fishing this A.M. Caught 10, weighing 17-3/4 lbs. This is the Grandest, Finest Sport I ever saw! Weather is quite nice and warm. Shower. Clouds but no rain. Mail came in from Ft. Fetterman. 2 letters from Penna. *[Pennsylvania]*, 1 from Ct. *[Connecticut]*. It seems very good to hear from civilization once more. Hot, fair weather.

June 27   Rained last night and this morning. Warm.

June 28   No news. Weather getting Hotter every day. Warm.

Camping along trout-filled creeks in the Black Hills provided hours of idle enjoyment and fresh food for George and other soldiers during the summer campaign of 1876. Here, soldiers pitch tents and make pine bough huts. Photograph by Stanley J. Morrow.

The field headquarters of Gen. George Crook at Whitewood, Dakota Territories, during the Black Hills Expedition of 1876. The camp scene shows tents improvised from wagon frames.

June 29 Moved camp up the Creek 1-1/2 miles. No News. Warm.

June 30 Rainy all day. Went fishing but did not get a bite, only from the Mosquitos. Got very wet. Warm.

July 1st Lying over. "B" Co's hunters saw 2 of the Enemy and killed one Bear. Warm.

July 2nd Went fishing. Caught 7 good, nice ones. Am getting fat and lazy. Wish I might have some of the Down Easters to eat with me.

July 3 No alteration.

July 4th Courier from Fetterman says *[wagon]* train will not be here for 12 or 14 days yet order consolidation with Terry sometimes I do not know when after the arrival of the train, I suppose.

July 5th Very hot.

July 6th Moved for Grazing 1-1/2 miles.

July 7th Bunky and I went fishing. Caught 21 Trout. Shot one Partridge. Wind blowing very hot. Light showers in the P.M. My Bunky and I ate all the Trout for supper. Hot.

July 8th Company exercise to keep the horses in good running condition. Hot but pretty comfortable today. Hot and fine weather.

July 9 One Pack Mule and One Horse stolen by Indians. The Infantry fired on them but don't know as they hit any of them. Lt. Sibley's party came in today. They were attacked by Indians some 100 miles from here and had to leave their Horses. They were found by a party of Hunters this Morning and food and Horses were sent

(PAGE 237)
out to them immediately. Cornwall of Company "D" became insane from fright and suffering. Fine weather.

[Lt. Frederick W. Sibley and 25 soldiers from the 2nd Cavalry escorted two scouts, Frank Grouard and Big Bat (Baptiste Pourier), to locate an Indian village near the head of the Little Big Horn River. Two Cheyenne braves were killed. The soldiers used their horses as bait and hiked back to camp on foot after evading the Indians. They returned to camp at 10 a.m. on July 9th. For further reading of the event, read Chapter 17 of the John S. Gray book, Centennial Campaign: The Sioux War of 1876, *and Jerome A. Greene's book,* Battles and Skirmishes of the Great Sioux War, 1876–1877: The Military View, *Chapter 5 by Baptiste Pourier. Lt. John G.*

Bourke noted in his daily diary, On the Border with Crook, *that two soldiers who were new recruits went crazy.]*

July 10   We had quite a battle last night, making 10 so far this summer. The Indians accomplished nothing but firing the Prairie which caused us some trouble. The Indians lost one man and one Pony. The Pack Mules returned with Elk meat, some 60 Elk. The Indians lost one man last night and one Pony. Today we heard of the last terrible fight of Col. Custer.

[Gen. Crook had left on July 7 to hunt with other soldiers. They returned the afternoon of July 10. Louis Richard and courier Ben Arnold arrived from Fort Fetterman telling of the Custer battle June 25 and 26. The Sioux burned at least one hundred miles of prairie pasture and generally bothered the camping troops for two weeks. Lt. John G. Bourke details the events in his diary.]

July 11th   Went out this morning with two Co's, "E" and "B" to Fort Phil Kearney. Scouted through the foothills but saw no Indians. Reached Kearney at 12:10. Fine. 14 miles.

July 12   Marched back to wood Camp but the train could not make it so we halted and camped at a Spring in the foothills. 16 miles.

[According to reports by Gen. Crook, the troops remained in the field for three weeks thinking they were outnumbered by the Indians when in fact only a handful of Indians remained on the plains after the Sibley skirmish.]

July 13   Camped last night 4 miles from Camp. Twiggs shot at a mouse. Came in to Camp this Morning. Courier from Terry is confirming the death of Custer's party. 256 men killed, I think. 213 Shoshones came in to act as scouts. Fine. 4 miles.

[On July 11, Lt. Bourke reported that 220 Shoshones under the direction of Chief Washakie arrived in camp. Lt. Bourke notes that the couriers were privates from Clifford's Company E named William Evans, Benjamin F. Stewart, and James Bell. Lt. Bourke reported that Col. Chambers arrived July 13, with seven companies of infantry and a wagon train loaded with supplies. Dr. V. T. McGillicuddy arrived with Col. Chambers. He is pictured in this book.]

July 14   Some showers today. Grand parade of Shoshones in full war dress.

[George's brief mention of the grand parade belies the extent of the demonstration by Shoshone warriors. Lt. Bourke described the grand parade on this day as an opportunity for the Shoshones to introduce new recruits to the Indian culture. The warriors wore warbonnets, bright blankets, scarlet cloth, head dresses of feathers, and gleaming rifles and lances. The braves rode bareback on spirited ponies, straight as arrows. On command by Chief Washakie, the warriors formed two columns, rode outside the camp, and raced at a furious gallop back to the amazed cavalry and infantry troops in a flourish of dust, pounding hoofs, and screeching Indian voices.]

July 15 No alteration. Fine.

July 16 Moved Camp 2 miles to a small Creek farther north (8:13 A.M.) Mail went out and I got letters away to folks East.

[Army records show that the men under the command of Gen. George Crook camped along Big Goose Creek in Northern Wyoming. Capt. King details his encounter with Cheyenne warriors on War Bonnet Creek in his daily diary, Campaigning with Crook, *as a senior officer under the command of Col. Wesley Merritt of the 5th Cavalry.]*

July 17 No alteration. Fine weather.

July 18 No alteration. Fine weather.

July 19 No alteration. Fine weather.

July 20 Dispatch from Gen'l Terry. Contents weeks old. Indians say the Little Big Horn is lined with Sioux dead from the Custer fight. Fine weather.

[Crow Indian scouts sat and with their fingers told of the Custer fight, the attack of Crazy Horse and Sitting Bull, and the stream of killed and wounded, according to Lt. Bourke.]

End of the 1st Book

July 21st Moved Camp today 3-1/2 miles to So. Fork of Tongue River. Hot. 3-1/2 miles.

July 22 No news in Camp. It is thought the Enemy are in the Big Horn Mts. North-west of here. Hot.

[Crook wrote to Gen. Sheridan that on Powder, Tongue, and Rosebud Rivers the whole country was on fire and filled with smoke. He was in constant dread of attack and was paralyzed to do anything, according to letters he filed regarding this campaign that were found in the National Archives. No scouts were sent out to check the facts on the location of the Sioux.]

July 23 On Piquet again found the most peculiar stone I ever saw. Hot. Showers.

July 24 Moved across So. Fork Tongue River and camped in the Mud. Rained nearly all the Afternoon and it made the day nice, I assure you. Fishing some

(PAGE 238)
today catching houndheads. Very fine eating. We are now within 65 miles of a large body of the Enemy, so the Scouts say, but we have got to wait for Ammunition and Reinforcements. The story is that 8 Co's of the 5th Cavalry accompanied by 4 Co's of Infantry are on the Road to join us. Rumor says we leave here for a fight the night of the 30th. Rain.

Soldiers butcher a horse on the Horsemeat or Starvation March of September 1876. George Howard wrote, "It is terrible. Nothing to eat but Horse-meat." Photograph by Stanley J. Morrow.

Weakened horses and mules were shot for food during the Big Horn Expedition as rations became short. George S. Howard noted that horses and mules began to be shot September 5, 1876, and continued being shot through September 13. Photograph by Stanley J. Morrow.

July 25   Rained nearly all day. Thunder showers. Shoshones report large body of warriors in the Mts. 2 or 3 miles from here. Rain.

[Lt. Bourke reported that Shoshones under Chief Washakie located a large camp of the enemy at the headwaters of the Little Big Horn and around the corner of the mountain to the canon of the Big Horn. Hundreds of lodges and thousands of ponies were found but the Shoshones said the Sioux were eating ponies and dogs. Another scouting party, led by Louis Richaud, passed over the Big Horn Mountains and into the canyon of the Big Horn River where they sighted evidence of Sioux movements.]

July 26   Col. Carr is expected today but has not arrived. Showery. Shoshones have all gone out to provoke a fight. Showery.

July 27   Moved Camp today 3 miles. Killed a deer in Camp today. We are now on the North Fork of Tongue River, I think, but do not know. Lots of Trout in the Creek. Fair. 3 miles.

July 28   Not very warm. Fine.

July 29   Not very warm. Fine.

July 30   Moved Camp this morning 2 miles west, nearer the Big Horn Mts. We're only 2 miles from the mts. now. Dead Indian in Camp killed by Lt. Sibley, it is thought.

July 31st   Hot today and windy. Some fires approaching. Fine. 2 miles.

Aug. 1st   Fire coming from the South from our old Camp. We are catching some of the finest Trout I ever saw weighing from 2 to 3 lbs. Indians reported down the Creek. The Indians came in from down the creek fishing and so wild a tale that all the horses were taken in and tied to the Picket Line and the men went to cleaning cartridges and it really looked like a Fight but no Enemy appeared.

[Maj. Orlando H. Moore, 6th U.S. Infantry, reported to the Secretary of War on August 4, 1876, that Indians attacked him and the men of the 6th and 17th Infantry who were on the Yellowstone River to retrieve supplies for George Howard's company and other cavalry units with Gen. Crook who camped along the Powder River. The Indians George reports were sighted on a creek on August 1, attacked Moore and the men on August 2, who were aboard the "Far West" steamer, the steamer George mentions in his diary as the one bringing food to his company. The complete report filed by Maj. Moore is found in Jerome A. Greene's book, Battles and Skirmishes of the Great Sioux War, 1876–1877: The Military View, *and from reports found in the National Archives by me.]*

Aug. 2nd   Hot with some wind. The 5th Cavalry expected tomorrow.

Aug. 3rd   Moved over on Goose Creek to our first Camp this morning. The 5th are some where but nobody knows where. 17 miles.

Aug. 4   Orders to start tomorrow for 15 days with 4 days Rations in the Saddle. Storm brewing in 2 ways. 17 miles.

[Gen. Crook reported that the number of troops included 1,800 soldiers, 250 Indian scouts, and 200 volunteers and packers. Lt. Bourke reported that each man received half rations of bacon, sugar, coffee, and salt and full rations of hard bread.]

Aug. 5   Had a Row this morning. Broke camp this A.M. at 6:30 and marched down Goose Creek to Tongue River, then down Tongue and finally camped on the Tongue in a very nice bottom. 23 miles.

[The surgeon assigned to this march, Bennett A. Clements, said few men were sick at this time but rain storms were making things uncomfortable.]

Aug. 6   Marched down the Tongue River through nice bottoms and again camped on the Tongue, crossed the River 17 times. 23 miles.

(PAGE 239)
Aug. 7th   Went from Tongue River over the divide to the Rosebud 29 miles. Reached the Rosebud some 13 or 14 miles below the Battlefield of June 17th. Dusty. Shoshones report 14 dead. Sioux just above here killed in our fight or in Gen'l Custer's.

Aug. 8th   Broke camp this A.M. at 7:30 and went about 1 mile and camped again. What for, I do not know. Large fire coming from the northwest. Started again this P.M. at 6 o'clock and marched down the Rosebud 17 miles. Signs of large Indian village all the way down the creek with plenty of evidence that the party camping here were in the Custer fight. Very hot. 18 miles total.

Aug. 9   Broke camp this morning in good season. Marched down the Rosebud today. The Country is very good in the Valleys but the Hills which are isolated Buttes are barren of anything but running Cedar. The top of the Buttes are Red Sand stone. It is hard and prevents the Buttes from wearing away by the action of the Elements. The bottom of the Buttes are Soft white sandstone and clay and are slowly crumbling away. There are many actions and signs of Volcanic Eruptions. 19 miles marched. Cloudy. Some Rain. Cold.

Aug. 10   Still marching down the Rosebud. Went past several rather fresh Indian graves and the remains of a large shed where a large Sundance had been held. There were six Buffalo Heads collected in the ring and a War pole in the center smeared with blood. Valley fine, wood small, mostly Choke cherry and Plum brush. Met Gen'l Terry's command consisting of the Remnants of the 7th Cavalry and 15 Co's of Infantry belonging to the 5th, 18th and 22nd, I believe. Drew rations from Terry's wagon train. His train was 200 wagons and they are using 7 steamers on the Yellowstone to bring up their "Needfuls." 21 miles.

[Marching with the men included William "Buffalo Bill" Cody, his friend and side-kick, Jonathan White "Buffalo Chips," Jack Russell, and Jack Crawford, the "Poet Scout." Temperatures were below zero and the troops carried no tents or extra blankets. Capt. Charles King in his diary, Campaigning with Crook, *provided these details.]*

Aug. 11th   Marched over to Tongue River. Found skeleton of white man in camp tonight. Had been killed for 2 years or so. The man had been shot in the back and scalped. 13 miles. Showery.

Aug. 12th   Lay over in camp the a.m. It rained nearly all night and almost all day. One Camp was in a big Cottonwood grove. Some very fine grass. Found out that 2 of my Friends were killed with Custer. Moved down Tongue River this P.M. 11 miles. Saturday. Rainy.

(PAGE 240)

Aug. 13th   Broke Camp at 7:30 A.M. and marched down to Tongue. The Road was very muddy and heavy. The Bottom was very fine, not very wide in some places. 25 miles. Fine.

[Terry's troops campaigned with many provisions. Crook's men campaigned with few comforts. George Howard makes no mention of sacrifice during the marches, but Lt. Bourke notes that the two general's and their troops were in stark contrast.]

Aug. 14   Left Camp at 7:30 and came down the Tongue 6 miles, then turned to the Right on a Creek unknown to me. *[Regimental reports list the creek as Pumpkin Creek or "Squashy Creek" to the troops.]* The signs of Indians are some 4 days old. The grazing is good, the grass being fine and heavy. Lots of Sagebrush and Greasewood, Cotton wood and Box Elder in the Bottoms. It rained up all night and that made it very disagreeable and the trail heavy, the soil being more or less clayey. Rain. 15 miles.

["The trail they were following seemed to be fresh but our Indian scouts disagreed," said Capt. King in his diary on August 14.]

Aug. 15   Left Camp this A.M. at 7 o'clock. Rained all night. Morning fine. The march today very slow through a very rough country devoid of water and nearly destitute of wood. The Road was over succession of ridges and very steep, yet this ground clayey. Camped on the Powder River and above the mouth of the Mizpah in one of the finest bottoms I ever saw. The Cotton wood look as though they had been planted in rows. Thunder showers as we were going to water. Showery. 19 miles.

Aug. 16th   Left Camp at 7 A.M. Road was fine. Thunder showers in the P.M. Camped tonight on the Powder in another fine bottom. Showery. 19 miles.

Aug. 17th   Did not rain last night for a wonder and today is the Indian's day. Started down the River. Crossed and went up on a Table Land, very pretty. Trail 11 by 8 miles. Lots of Indians. Trail going East. The trail looks like a big square trail, they having wounded warriors on trevoy's. Camped tonight on the Yellowstone *[River]*. There is a steamer coming down the River. *[Steamer was the "Far West" which was delayed, according to Capt. King.]* The first I have seen since 1872 and it seems queer to see one here. One of those blue spells of mine seems to be on me tonight and out here away from the noise of Camp better thoughts seem floating o'er the hardened case and my childhood Home seems in plain sight and vividly memory brings back each incident and Heaven that I seldom think of seems far nearer than Earth. Most tritely does that Scriptural passage occur to me, "I will keep them in the hollow of my hand." The Crows were right. We are more than two weeks away from the Sioux we are tracking. 18 miles. Fine.

Aug. 18th   Lay over. Drew green coffee. It would seem as though this was roughing it in earnest to friends in the

(PAGE 241)
East with only a spoon, tin cup and knife be expected to parch Coffee. Fine.

Aug.19th   Lay over in camp on Yellowstone. Moved in the P.M. 1/2 mile.

Aug. 20   Lying over. Fine.

Aug. 21   Lying over. Train from the Rosebud coming in on the North Bank of the River. Fine weather.

Aug. 22   Rained last night and nearly all day today. No News. Rain.

[George's brief entry belies the severe weather pattern that Lt. Bourke describes in his August 22nd entry. "No stringing together of words can complete a description of what we saw, suffered, and feared during that awful tempest. The stoutest hearts, the oldest soldiers, quailed . . . There was scarcely a day from then on for nearly a month that my note-books do not contain references to storms."]

Aug. 23   Cloudy in the P.M. Saw McCarthy. He has been all through the States since his discharge. Been to the Centennial *[Celebrations for the 100-year anniversary of the United States was held in Philadelphia.]* Moved up the River 1 mile. Rained all night tonight. Cloudy.

[Surgeon Moore reported that on this day 34 sick and disabled men were sent to the "Far West" for treatment of "acute dysentery and diarrhea." The storm George mentions was so fierce that no one slept, according to Capt. King and Surgeon Moore. ". . . a most violent storm of rain and wind occurred, rendering sleep impossible, and saturating everything with water," wrote Moore.]

Aug. 24   Marched up the Powder 9 miles. Showery and Cold in the morning. Fair in the P.M.

Aug. 25   Marched up the River 17 miles. Terry came up to Camp with news of the Indians, I think.

[In fact, Gen. Terry attempted to resupply Crook's column but Crook left and sent his troops up river before the steamer, "Far West," could land. Lt. Charles B. Scholfield gave Terry's letter to Muggins Taylor who found Crook and his troops moving 17 miles from camp. Terry had not been informed of the movement, according to Capt. King.]

Aug. 26   Left Powder River and started across the country toward the Little Missouri Country. Fair. No Wood or Water. Plenty of Sage Hens in Camp. 22 miles.

[Gen. Crook thought he was on the trail of Indians but had followed a path created by Gen. Terry's engineers in the spring according to John Gray in his book, Centennial Campaign: The Sioux War of 1876.*]*

Aug. 27   Marched across country toward the Little Missouri. Crossed Beaver Creek. *[Beaver Creek runs through mideastern Montana near present-day Carlyle and Saint Phillip and flows into midwestern North Dakota near present-day Trotters.]* Fine stream. Taken sick. 19 miles.

[Cold, rainy weather and poor food supplies added to the sacrifice of the troops and increased the number of soldiers who became ill. Reporters on the march noted that men suffered from scurvy, dysentery, and rheumatism.]

Aug. 28th   Marched East, 28 miles. Crossed one creek and camped on the Glendive. Camped in the sage brush and Clayey ground and then came up a fine Shower accompanied by hail and it made things fine, you bet. Hail stones fell as large as Hen's eggs. 28 miles.

[Lt. Bourke reported in his diary that the hail arrived at 4 p.m. The herds of horses and mules were frightened and the temperatures continued to drop, adding to the misery of the troops. A

This is one of the methods used to carry wounded men after the Battle of Slim Buttes, Dakota Territories. Photograph by Stanley J. Morrow.

Officers of the 3rd Cavalry pause after the Battle of Slim Buttes in front of a captured Indian lodge. Custer's guidon was recovered during the Battle of Slim Buttes. George S. Howard noted, "A great many things were recognized as belonging to the 7th Cavalry showing that those Indians had been in that fight." Photograph by Stanley J. Morrow.

bolt of lightning struck in camp, setting fire to the grass on a post near the sentinel. The men had gone without sleep due to the continuing rain and low temperatures, he wrote.]

Aug. 29th   Started East today. The Rain of last night made travelling difficult. Morning fine. Camped at Sentinel Buttes. I was pretty sick today. Gen'l Terry's train should meet us here with 10 or 12 days Rations. 7 miles.

[Lt. Bourke said detachments of hunters were sent out to bring in fresh wild game of deer, antelope, and jackrabbits for the sick. The men suffered from neuralgia, rheumatism, malaria, and diarrhea. Lt. Huntington could not sit on his horse and Lt. Bache had to be carried on a travois. Enlisted men fended for themselves as best they could, Capt. King said.]

Aug. 30   Moved South one mile. Very sick. Wednesday. 1 mile.

[Grace Howard Porter, daughter of Moccasin Joe, remembered hearing of the great sacrifice her father made during this march. He would often repeat hair-raising tales of illness and starvation until her mother would beg George to stop scaring the girls.]

Aug. 31st   Moved about 10 miles North this Morning and made a halt but I think we move again before night. McManus of "D" Company bit by a Rattlesnake. The doctor, Surgeon Patzki, burned the wound and poured ammonia on it. McManus enjoyed whiskey to kill the pain. He will live. Marched 10 miles. Cold. No blankets, no tent and clothing soaked. What a miserable life.

[So cold were the temperatures that Lt. Bourke said several of Gen. Crook's officers and several enlisted men nearly froze to death. Extra supplies from Terry had not arrived because Crook had not kept in touch. Scouts explored the Glendive and Beaver Creeks and the Little Missouri. This river is located in the southeastern corner of Montana near present-day Alzada as well as northeastern Wyoming and the Dakotas. Surgeon Moore said Beaver Creek was pure to drink and the cases of illness began to decline, especially when soldiers found berries to eat.]

Sept. 1st   Moved North 8 miles. Country rolling. Timber, none. Grass and Water good and plenty. 8 miles.

Sept. 2nd   Moved down the Creek today. I am getting better but was very sick yesterday. 21 miles.

Sept. 3rd   Moved out to the East this morning. Weather fine. No wood nor water. Camped tonight on the Little

(PAGE 242)
Missouri in Fine Camp. Lots of berries. 17 miles.

Troops move past an abandoned stockade beside French Creek, Dakota Territories. George S. Howard wrote that the troops camped on French Creek above Custer City September 23, 1876. Photograph by Stanley J. Morrow.

Cavalry troops leave Custer City during the Big Horn Expedition in 1876. George S. Howard marched to Custer City on French Creek September 23 and wrote, "It is a large mining city but partly deserted. There are houses enough for 3,000 inhabitants." Supplies for the expedition were left at Custer City. Camp Collins became Custer City.

Sept. 4th   Camped last night. It is a fine Stream, well wooded. Marched through some rough Country today. Made a long march. Party of Soldiers came in on the other side of the River. I do not know who they were. Courier went in tonight. Half Rations. that lets me out. 28 miles.

[This was the day Gen. Terry decided to abandon his unsuccessful campaign against the Sioux. Supplies for Gen. Crook's men were to be at Glendive, not Fort Buford. Lt. Bourke reported that Gen. Crook decided to guide troops to the gold mining town of Deadwood, 175 miles away and away from immediate supplies.]

Sept. 5   Marched East 20 miles and Camped on Green River. 20 Miles.

[Camp was struck about 100 miles west of Fort Abraham Lincoln in present-day North Dakota. Fort Lincoln was established on June 14, 1872, on the right bank of the Missouri River at the mouth of the Heart River to protect Northern Pacific Railroad workers. It was near present-day Bismarck. The fort was abandoned in July of 1891, and is a part of the state park system off of Interstate 94.]

Sept. 6   First day on 1/2 Rations. Marched South 33 miles and Camped at Milk Pond in a Table Land devoid of wood. I do not know where we are going but should think it about time to go Home.

[The lake was alkali near Rainy Buttes. Troops began shooting and eating ailing horses and mules, Capt. King and Lt. Bourke reported on this day. This is the beginning of the famous "Horsemeat March of 1876."]

Sept. 7th   Marched 33 miles South today. No wood, poor water. 1/2 Rations after making Camp. Capt. Mills, 3rd Cav., started with 160 men and part of the Pack Train for Deadwood settlement, Black Hills, to obtain Rations for the command. Very wet weather. Clothing and Blankets all wringing wet.

[Capt. Anson Mills selected 15 of his best-mounted men from ten companies of the 3rd Cavalry. Tom Moore was in charge of a pack train and Frank Grouard and Jack Crawford were guides. Dr. Stevens and reporters Strahorn and Davenport went with the the rescue column. Mills' military records record the details of his march to Deadwood.]

Sept. 8th   Marched South to better water and a little wood. Raining still. Issued for Rations 1/2 Coffee, 1/2 Hard Bread, and Horse meat. This is a fine food for men in a civilized Country.

[Grouard returned in a hurry that afternoon to say Indians were spotted at Slim Buttes.]

Sept. 9th   Rained nearly all night. Had marched about 15 miles when news was received that Capt. Mills had had a fight. A portion of the Command was hurried forward and by the time we arrived they had captured a village of 36 Teepees, 150 Ponies

Photograph courtesy of National Archives.

Deadwood was a rip-roaring place when George S. Howard rode through town in 1875 and 1876. While in the Black Hills he patrolled for miners and hunted for elk and deer.

and best of all some 2-1/2 tons of Dried Meat! This was a Godsend considering the reduced circumstances of our commissariat.

We Picketed the Horses and went to the Village to see what was to be seen. The Indians must have been well prepared for the Winter. Besides the Meat, they had immense quantities of Dried berries and Plums already put up in bags for transportation or use and Buffalo Robes in Abundance. Their lodges or Teepees were made of the finest Tanned Buffalo skins. The Village was attacked at 4 A.M. and completely surprised in consequence of which they had no time to remove anything. We found a great many articles used in civilization, among the collection

(PAGE 243)

almost every article used by the Housewife in the Kitchen and a great many things recognized as belonging to the 7th Cavalry showing that those Indians had been in that fight *[Battle at the Little Big Horn, June 25 and 26, 1876]*. At the time we arrived, the Indians had all been driven out with the exception of a few who had taken refuge in a Ravine about 55 ft. deep running into the side of a hill and so thickly covered with brush that they were completely hidden from sight. From there they had killed 1 and wounded two of our men. Killed Buffalo Chips *[friend of Buffalo Bill Cody]*. Some 5 or 6 sharpshooters lay waiting for a chance at them but they were careful not to expose themselves. They finally were got out by some of the Guides who could talk their language, they telling them that they would not be harmed. 13 then came out and gave themselves up. The Indians came in again in the Evening and wounded 2 men of the 5th Cavalry, one of them so bad that he died before morning.

[Excellent details of the battle are found in Capt. King's daily diary. Lt. Bourke also gives a detailed account of the battle. The private who died was Kennedy of Company C, Fifth Cavalry, according to King.]

Sept. 10th Piquets fired occasionally all night and the Indians came around this Morning but hurt no one. The 5th Cavalry laid for them and killed 9, besides wounding others, the No. *[number]* unknown. Wood and water getting more plenty. It is very cold, disagreeable weather and all we get to eat is some Horse Meat, using the Horses that are playing out and 1/2 lb. dried meat per day. Showery. 12 miles.

Sept. 11th Moved toward the Black Hills in the direction of Deadwood. Nothing to eat but Horse Meat. Rain. 25 miles.

Sept. 12 Still pointing for the Hills. Very bad today and the horses all playing out. It is terrible. Nothing to eat but Horse-meat. Camped tonight on Owl Creek and began to get to where a man has been. 41 miles. Rain.

[The men marched toward Bear Butte and into the Black Hills with few provisions. This butte is near present-day Sturgis, South Dakota, and is 4,422-feet high. A state park is located in

Officers' wives and the issuing agent distribute flour to reservation Indians at Camp Supply, Indian Territory. Indians became dependent upon agencies for their food and shelter after their way of life was destroyed by the white men.

the same area today. One man was killed when he left the march without permission to hunt for antelope. He was killed by a band of Sioux following the troops. Lt. Bourke said the march was 41 miles and they camped on Willow Creek. No wood was found.]

Sept. 13 Moved over on the Belle-Fourche *[River]* at noon. Our Good Luck is coming. It has cleared up so that things are getting dry. Some men who went for Rations on the 11th have returned and say we will get rations tonight. I have seen some Hard Bread they brought with them. This makes 6 days on Horse-meat. If this is Soldiering, I have got through. 7 miles.

[A herd of 50 cattle and supply trains entered camp after noon. Rain had drenched the men for 22 days, so the sun of this day was much appreciated. Capt. King reported that half the men in the march did not come into camp until noon due to the rains of September 12, and their lack of energy brought on by starvation and physical sacrifice.]

(PAGE 244)
Sept. 14th Lay over on the Belle Fourche. A fine, nice day. Every good and plenty to eat.

[All the bacon, coffee and flour from Crook City and Deadwood arrived at 5 p.m. Warm blankets also arrived, adding to the general comforts of the soldiers, according to Capt. King.]

Sept. 15th Moved to a fine trout stream. Lots of every thing but bacon. Weather fine. Country very good for farming. 7 miles.

[Troops enjoyed their first taste of vegetables and beef in many weeks. The food brought a welcome relief to their sacrifice and thoughts of suffering faded, according to Capt. King. The march without provisions that George and Capt. King describe has become known as "The Horsemeat March of 1876." George's brief entries indicate the level of suffering he was experiencing. King said the men had little energy to do anything because of illness and hunger. The monthly reports of George's company did not appear in the National Archives as had all the other monthly entries. In the personnel files of commanding officers, such as Crook, reports of the events and marches did exist.]

Sept. 16th Lay over. The Rations were issued double today so we now have plenty to eat.

Sept. 17 Moved up stream. Fine, fair day. Plenty of grass, wood and water. Fine country. We are now on White-Wood Creek. 4 miles.

[Troops camped on the Whitewood and Deadwood Creeks. Gen. Crook was ordered by Gen. Sheridan to meet for a conference at Fort Laramie, so he and his officers left the troops and stayed in Deadwood before heading for Fort Laramie. The Big Horn and Yellowstone Expeditions officially ended a month later. Troops were now under the command of Gen. Merritt.]

Sept. 18   Moved up past Crook City onto the Centennial Group as of Black Hills fame. Crook City is on Dead Wood Creek. It is a town of some 1000 inhabitants. It has some 20 Stores, a Billiard Room, 2 Meat Markets, Milk Wagons running and 2 Bakeries. The Indians bother them a great deal here coming almost into town and stealing stock. Water a long way off. Wood the same but plenty. 11 miles.

Sept. 19   Moved up Deadwood Creek taking the Road to Custer City. Morning Cold. Crossed Elder and Badwood Creeks. Country hilly and very finely wooded. No grass. Plenty of wood and water. Made 26 miles and at Box Elder Creek (Mountain Meadow) met 1 co. of 4th Artillery with supplies for us. They had come some 200 miles nearly in 7 days hearing we were starving. 26 miles.

[Commander of the 4th Artillery was Capt. Frank Guest Smith. Horses received oats and corn for the first time in months, King reported.]

Sept. 20   Lay over at Mountain Meadow. Weather fine.

Sept. 21st   Moved south to Rapid Creek, 13 miles. Stopped at Camp Crook so named in 1875 by Col. Dodges Expedition. Weather fine. Wood and Water fine and plenty. Met Capt. Egan and detachment of Company "K", 2nd Cav'y with Empty Wagons for our wounded, they having left supplies at Custer City for us. They have no news except that the 4th Cav'y is at Red Cloud and some of the 4th Art.

[Egan gave his fresh horses to Crook and his men to reach Fort Laramie in time for his meeting with Sheridan according to Lt. Bourke. Rapid Creek flows through present-day Rapid City, South Dakota. Their camping location was within a few miles of present-day Mount Rushmore National Monument that celebrated its 50th anniversary in 1991.]

Sept. 22   Moved over to Spring Creek 17 miles. Weather fine. Wood & Water good and plenty.

(PAGE 245)
Camped tonight near Hill City and used mining city near the mouth of Newton Fork. Camped at what one year ago was the best hunting place in the Hills. We are now in country that I am perfectly at home in, knowing it thoroughly.

[George spent all of 1875 horseback riding in the Black Hills near Deadwood, according to Army records. He was on a detachment of scouts who were responsible for controlling the influx of miners into Black Hill gold camps. The effort by the Army didn't work, and white men overwhelmed the area.]

Sept. 23   Marched to Custer City off French Creek. It is a large mining City but partly deserted. There are houses enough for 3000 inhabitants. Another Train up from Red Cloud. 12 miles.

Sept. 24   Lay over on French Creek just above Custer City. Every thing quiet. Rec'd Letters from So. Boston. Sent letters to Poquonock and So. Berwick, Mass.

Sept. 25   Moved up the Creek 2 miles. Rumor is Good Indians been disarmed at the Agency. The Rest go on the Warpath. They say our Train left Ft. Laramie yesterday for here. There has been no Rain in the Hills this Summer and water is scarce. Wild Bill Hickox was killed some 20 days ago at Deadwood City.

[Wild Bill Hickock and Calamity Jane are buried in Deadwood.]

Sept. 26   Rumor is Indians want peace. Lay over.

Sept. 27   Moved down the Creek 3-1/2 miles to more water and better grass. One man of "B" Company 2nd *[Cav.]* died today in Hospital.

Sept. 28   Lay over, Cloudy.

Sept. 29   Lay over. Cleared up. Mail from the train came in. 2 from Conn. *[Connecticut]*, 1 from Auburn, 1 from Mass. *[Massachusetts]* Sent Home one and one to North Adams.

[Capt. King said in his diary, "Once in a while letters began to reach us from anxious ones at home and make us long to see them; and yet no orders came, no definite prospects of relief from our exile." The troops stayed on French Creek several weeks until October 23, when they were at Red Cloud Agency to take part in the closing part of the 1876 campaign.]

Sept. 30   Lay over. Weather fine. Getting cold nights. The Bugs are getting into the Command.

[King reported that bed bugs, fleas and other uncomfortable insects that bit soldiers made their home in blankets, socks, and anything that lay close to the skin of soldiers.]

Oct 1st   Lay Over. We all went out looking for a New Camp on the Red Cloud Road. We have made 75.2 miles since leaving Wagon Train the 5th of August. Killed between here and Fort Sanders 6 Rabbits and one Sage Cock at 7 shots. Arrived at Fort Sanders Nov 4th after being out 8 mos. and 19 days and in the Saddle 2600 miles, a pretty fair summer campaign.

[Capt. King wondered how the men had stood the hardships of the campaign noting that many suffered from rheumatism from the harsh conditions of rain and marching.]

(PAGE 246)

[George S. Howard copied a poem on this page titled, "Of Such as I Have," by Susan Cooledge which is not translated here and the following untitled poem that is by George S. Howard. The untitled poem was at the end of the diary and probably was written in January of 1877, five months before George's enlistment ended. From Fort Sanders, George returned to his mother in Hinsdale, New Hampshire.]

> *My time here in the Army*
> > *Thank God is almost done*
> *Yet the days seem longest now*
> > *So anxious am I to get Home*
> *I've put my time in bravely*
> > *And tried to do my best*
> *Have always done my duty*
> > *Always done as much as the rest*
>
> *Yet I am getting terribly tired*
> > *And long to get away*
> *Although I must go to work*
> > *With no time at all to play*
> *But I am so tired of the brutality*
> > *So often displayed toward the ranks*
> *And I long once more to be wandering*
> > *Mid New England's mossy banks.*

(PAGE 247)

> *Yet it's only five months or so*
> > *Till I again shall be free*
> *And safe away on the road*
> > *Toward that far away Countrie*
> *But I'll try to do my duty*
> > *As long as I have to stay*
> *Do nothing for which I'll be sorry*
> > *When at Home so faraway.*
>
> > > > *Moccasin Joe*

FRIENDSHIP

We met as friends on Life's Dark Stream
And the hours since then have passed like a dream
We vied with each other who most could do
To keep Friendship's chain forever in view
I am glad that I met you as I journeyed along
When my life was all prose with never a song
You have taught me how life far better might be
As we journey on toward Eternity
You have showed me how life though shrouded in gloom
Should ne'er be a Funeral march toward the tomb.
We met, loved and must part as others have done
Yet we'll cherish this time when asunder welcome
We must say good-bye but we cannot forget yet
That the hours passed together were Happiest
Now the parting must come, we must e'er say adieu
And press onward again with this Friendship in verse.

> *Moccasin Joe*
> *to Johanna Erkisson from Denmark*
> *at Laramie City*

5/21/78

(PAGE 248)

As I've nothing else to do I will tonight recall the Young Ladies of my acquaintance.

1.	Mifs	Rosie Richmond	Hinsdale, N.H.	Married Robertson
2.	"	Ella K. Richmond	"　　"	My Marriage to her in paper January 1871
3.	"	Gertie Brockway	"　　"	Married Davis
4.	"	Cynthia Tollis	"　　"	Married Mike
5.	"	Augusta Hooker	"　　"	
6.	"	Emma Liscomb	"　　"	Married
7.	"	Mary Casey	"　　"	Married McCatherine
8.	"	Delia Weeks	Winchester "	Died Jan 1873
9.	"	Rose Battles	Hinsdale "	Married Snow
10.	"	Emma Higgins	"　　"	
11.	"	Rose Burfee	"　　"	
12.	"	Gertie Davenport	"　　"	
13.	"	Stella Handy	"　　"	Married Hunter
14.	"	Amelia Handy	"　　"	
15.	"	Addie Newton	"　　"	Married Gilmore
16.	"	Ida Eaton	"　　"	True Friend
17.	"	Eva Eaton	"　　"	True Friend Died December 1874, broken heart
18.	"	Carrie Taylor	"　　"	
19.	"	Isabel Palmer	"　　"	Married Whipple
20.	"	Emma Leason	"　　"	
21.	"	Addie Barnes		
22.	"	Ellen Lyons	Chesterfield, N.H.	Married
23.	"	Emma Durling	Winchester "	
24.	"	Mattie Epley	"　　"	
25.	"	Helen Baker	"　　"	Married Jim Spencer
26.	"	Laura Baker	"　　"	
27.	"	Helen Smith	"　　"	
28.	"	Laura Lyman	Northfield, Mass.	Mrs. E. O. Hale
29.	"	Lizzie Fulton	"　　"	Married—her father
30.	"	Fidelia Newton	"　　"	Married Trishel
31.	"	Minnie Mason	"　　"	Married Leonard Smith
32.	"	Mary and Mattie Long, twins	"　　"	Married Judson and McClur
33.	"	Angie Holton	"　　"	
34.	"	Francie Holton	"　　"	Died Feb 1873
35.	"	Estelle Wright	"　　"	
36.	"	Ann Wright	"　　"	
37.	"	Addie Wright	"　　"	

(PAGE 249)

38.	Mifs	Georgia Webster	Northfield, Mass.	
39.	"	Alice Dunklin	" "	Married Lyman
40.	"	Isabel Tolman	" "	Married Baud
41.	"	Gracie Creigh	Millers Falls	Married
42.	"	Mary Hubbard	" "	Married Stylis
43.	"	Lizzie Britt	" "	
44.	"	Fannie Britt	Greenfield, Mass.	
45.	"	Carrie Britt	" "	
46.	"	Carrie Jones	" "	
47.	"	Jennie Tyler	" "	
48.	"	Mary Tyler	" "	Died August 1872
49.	"	Ella Geirnan	" "	
50.	"	Mary Collins	" "	
51.	"	Julia Dare	" "	Married Ellit
		(Sophronia)		Died Sept 1876
52.	"	Kate Reed	" "	Married Hawks
53.	"	Kate Newton	" "	Married Wiley
54.	"	Bell Newton	" "	
55.	"	Emma Newton	" "	
56.	"	Sarah Newton	" "	
57.	"	Mary Newton	" "	Married Nash
58.	"	Ellen Sawtell	" "	Married Potter
59.	"	Carrie Hayward	" "	Married Blake
60.	"	Lilphia Thayer	" "	Married Livermore
61.	"	Ellen Arms	" "	Married
62.	"	Tillie Lewis	" "	Married Harding
63.	"	Carrie Weinech	" "	H. L. Miller
64.	"	Minnie Wells	" "	
65.	"	Ella Hull	" "	
66.	"	Emma Gatchell	Fitchburg, Mass.	Married
67.	"	Mary Downs	" "	
68.	"	Josephine Spring	Windsor Locks, Conn.	
69.	"	Fannie Abby	" "	
70.	"	Abby Harrington	" "	
71.	"	S. A. Loomis	Windsor, Conn.	Married April 1872
72.	"	Mary Clapp	" "	
73.	"	Lottie Phelps	" "	Married this spring to Dave Marshall
74.	"	Etta Griswold	" "	
75.	"	Mary Phelps	" "	Married
76.	"	Katie Phelps	" "	Married
77.	"	Carrie Smith	Glatonbury	

(PAGE 250)

78.	Mifs	Gorgie Allen	Windsor, Conn.	
79.	″	Cornelia Andrus	″ ″	
80.	″	Ella Kinney	″ ″	
81.	″	Celia Kenney	″ ″	
82.	″	Emogene Loomis	″ ″	Married Kinney
83.	″	Mattie Palmer	″ ″	Died June 1872
84.	″	Mary Kirkbride	″ ″	
85.	″	Delia Day	Orange, Mass.	Married Weeks
86.	″	Annie Martin	″ ″	Married
87.	″	Albertina Burnett	″ ″	Married
88.	″	Melissa Phinney	″ ″	
89.	″	Irene Foster	Athol, Mass.	Married Stenson
90.	″	Adah Clark	″ ″	
91.	″	Josie Strong	Palmyra, Wis.	
92.	″	Daisy Chadwick	Peoria, Ill.	Married Moccasin Joe
				Fact?
93.	″	Hester Plimell	London, Ohio	Died Jan 1874
94.	″	Amanda Swenson	Fort Laramie, Wyo.	Married Prachin
95.	″	Alice Brown	″ ″ ″	
96.	″	Lucy A. Low	North Adams, Mass.	Married Richardson
97.	″	Lizzie B. Barnes	Lee ″	Married Joe Reynolds
98.	″	Ellen Lane	Fitchburg ″	Married
99.	″	Mattie Goodrich	″ ″	
100.	″	Effie S. Packard	Ashburnham ″	Married Billings

That is enough to recall to mind, I guess. Oh, no. just one more —C.O.P.
Howard E Company, 2nd Cav'y.

101.	Mifs	Mary Donahue	Saratoga Precinct,	Omaha, Neb.
102.	″	Carrie O'Patrick	Saratoga Precinct,	Omaha, Neb.
103.	″	Mary E. Low	North Adams, Mass.	
104.	″	Annie M. Harris	Pittston, Penn.	
105.	″	Ellen M. McDuffee	So. Boston, Mass.	No. 4 Ward St. So. Berwick, Me.
106.	″	Addis L. Fisher	North Adams, Mass.	Box 157
107.	″	Elizabeth Stevens	Laramie City, Wyoming	
108.	″	Julie Cayle	″ ″ ″	
109.	″	Mate Ramsey	″ ″ ″	
110.	″	T. P. Johnson	″ ″ ″	
111.	″	Annie Hamilton	″ ″ ″	
112.	″	Nellie Wright	″ ″ ″	
113.	″	Emma Brannagan	″ ″ ″	
114.	″	Amanda Dunn	″ ″ ″	
115.	″	Rose McKenzie	Omaha, Neb.	

[Pages 251 and 252 missing from from original diary.]

(PAGE 253)

    Married on or about the 28th of January 1877. Mr. George S. Howard of Hinsdale, N.H. to Mrs. Lizzie Stevens of Boston, Mass. *[To the best of our knowledge this marriage did not take place. His only legal marriage was to Martha Colburn in 1879.]* Something queer about this winter I have been engaged to be married to two different women and both have fallen through.

Howard
known as Reynolds

Lizzie Roach	Omaha, Neb.
Jennie Porter	〞 〞
Josie Washburne	〞 〞
Q. C. Mundill	〞 〞
Alice S. Jones	Greenfield, Mass.
Addie Waliath	Vepepth, N.Y.

[Signature portions cut from stationary of various women who wrote to George out West.]

From your friend,	Ever Your Friend,
Libbie Loomis	Annie May Harris
Your sister May,	I am Respectfully
	Your Friend, I trust,
Miss May	
	Ella M. McDuffee

Married Jan 22nd 1879
    Mr. Geo. S. Howard and Martha Colburn of Chesterfield
    [This was George's first and only marriage.]

(PAGE 254)

Omaha, Neb. 1875

To anyone who will take the trouble to read this book and get the correct reading of the mistakes, they will find many nice pieces of poetry and some of prose.

I have endeavored to write nothing but what the most respectable of women may read. It has been my companion many a weary night and has kept me from growing worse and sinking deeper in vice than I was when I entered the Army.

Pieces of my own composition are marked Moccasin Joe (my nom-de-plume).

Hoping the recipient will appreciate the book and look at it in the pleasant and quiet hours of twilight and evening.

I will Remain Your Friend.

> Respectfully,
>
> Geo. Howard
> Company E, 2nd Cavalry
> Omaha Bks, Neb.

Residence
  Hinsdale
    Cheshire Company
      New Hampshire

My favorites are on pages 1, 8, 25, 31, 34, 44, 55, 60, 74, 77, 78, 80, 82, 84, 90, 94, 108, 114, 119, 120, 126, 129, 130, 133, 139, 146.

Sitting Bull, a Hunkpapa Sioux, was born in 1834 at Grand River, Dakota Territories, and died in 1890 while resisting arrest. He was known for performing in Buffalo Bill's Wild West Show. At the height of his power in 1876, Sitting Bull commanded 5,000 warriors. By 1881 he had only 160 followers.

[The following remedies were given to George S. Howard by Indians he knew while stationed in Wyoming, Montana, and South Dakota. His daughter said that the famous chief, Sitting Bull, may have been the one to give George these mixtures, but this is unlikely and cannot be confirmed. He may have used these treatments himself during his stay in the West.

George apparently had frequent spells because of a serious head injury incurred while working on the railroad prior to his enlistment in the Army. He mentions he was sick only a few times in his diary. The metal plate that doctors had inserted into his head in 1870 continued to cause extreme pressure and pain for him throughout his life. By the time he returned to his home in New Hampshire in 1877, George was dizzy and disoriented. His daughter said he had "fits" that would last several days. He and his wife separated a year before his murder because of his irregular behavior, Grace said.

The medicine remedies were faded which indicates to me they were well-worn pages in the diary that George turned to frequently. Translation of these pages was very difficult, so some of the spellings of words might be incorrect. Please excuse me. I tried to understand the words by holding the pages under a light and using a magnifying glass.]

Coughs

Equal Parts Sugar and Vinegar. Take one Tea spoonful every time the Cough occurs.

Ingrown Toenails

Shave the top of the Nail as thin as possible every Saturday. Regularly.

(PAGE 255)
[No use given in diary for the following remedy.]
  2 oz. Balsam Coparten
  2 oz. Swt. Oils Mtic.
  2 drops Oil Juniper
  2 drops _____ Iron
  2 drops turpentine

1 table spoonful, 20 minutes after eating breakfast.

Corns

  1 dr. croton oil
  1 dr. Oil spike
  1 dr. Olehs hot
  1 dr. Olive oil
  1 dr. Iodine of Iron

Small Pox

1 gr. Sulphate of Lyine
1 gr. Foxglove Digitalis
1/2 T. Spoonful Sugar
2 Table spoonfuls of water

When thoroughly mixed, add 4 oz. Table spoonful, every hour. For children, give according to age.

Consumption

Gather Mulliur leaves prior to the last of July. Dip in water. Make strong and drink freely.

Nose Bleed

Press the Thumb or Finger on the Artery passing over the jaw bone through a small indentation near the back teeth. By feeling on the Jaw the location may be distinguished.

Croup

Catch a Green Frog and place in hot skillet with 1/2 lb. Fresh butter. The frog alive— put on the cover and cook 20 minutes. Give T. spoonful as often as required.

Dysentery

Cherry Brandy, drink freely

Heart Burn

Parched coffee. Drink down.

Headache

Carry Rattlesnakes rattle on inside of the Hat. 1 pint bay rum and 1 oz. ammonia. 1 pint water. shake and rub well.

Coughs

Indian turnip, grated in honey, 1 teaspoonful before retiring.

(PAGE 256)

Scenes and incidents to be brought to Mind on Return to the States.
1st   The Finding of Lieut. Robinson's Body
2nd   The Trip to the Heart of the Indian Country
3rd   Being shot at by Lion and Recruit of 3rd. at Horseshoe
4th   Indian Chiefs' Names
        Brule Sioux, Sitting Bull, Red Cloud, Spotted Tail, Little Bear, Man afraid of his horse, Dull Knife, Old Crow. Arapahoe - Friday, Sly Fox, Raven Wing.

Dakota delegation that traveled to Washington, D.C., in 1875 included (standing l–r) Julius Meyer, a trader, and Red Cloud, the Oglala Chief. (Sitting l–r), Sitting Bull, not the famous Sioux leader; Swift Bear, an Arapaho chief; and Spotted Tail, a Brule chief. Photograph by Frank F. Currier.

Red Cloud, a great Oglala chief, was as a strong supporter of peace. It was said he and his warriors wore red blankets and paint and looked like a red cloud when they attacked. He stood more than 6-feet with piercing eyes and stoic expression.

Lizzie Bradley, Omaha, Neb.
Read by Jennie V. McCoy
Saratoga, Neb. June 8

Good-bye old book. Many an hour you've helped to pass away.

Moccasin Joe

Darling,

Well, Little One, have you looked it through, and if so, don't you think that the one who wrote it is not all bad?

Howard

(PAGE 257)

You would like to know who the owner of this book is. Well, he is Joe Reynolds of Greenfield, Mass.

Fort Sanders, Wyoming
May 14th, 1877

Of all the women I have known, I must not forget that Miss Johanna DeLindi or Erkisson is the one that has been more to me than any other.

Joe Reynolds

James W. Howard   Mr. Wm. A. Colton
Company E, 8th Volunteer   West Sowerville, Mass.
Ship Island

[James W. Howard was George's older brother who also served in the Civil War. Wm. A. Colton could not be identified, but the assumption is that he was a friend. Colton may have been George's hunting partner in the West who is photographed with George in 1872. Joe Reynolds was the commanding officer at the Battle of Powder River. George adopts Joe Reynolds as a name towards the end of the diary. The Powder River battle made a lasting and horrifying impression upon George. He wrote seven pages of poems about the incident from pages 193 to 200 in the diary. The women listed on the last page of the diary must have been favorite girlfriends, and from the list he gave us, he had plenty.]

Chapter Four

Poems by Moccasin Joe:
Reflections of Life on the Plains

The following is a section of George S. Howard's diary that is dedicated to poems and speeches. We have taken the liberty to delete all the poems and passages that were not penned by George. We have reproduced all those that were signed by George, or one of his noms-de-plume (e.g., Wild Dan, Moccasin Joe, M.J., Scar Head, Scar Head the Crazy Scout).

We have listed only the names of the poems and passages that were attributed to someone else, if mentioned, in George's diary. Research about the diary led us to believe that George spent many hours recalling favorite poems and speeches and copying them at the Fort Laramie library. He used the poems to pass away long hours and to bring comfort to him as he witnessed the horror of war and the destruction of the West. He had memorized favorite poems as a child and recorded them on the pages of his diary so he could carry a library with him throughout his enlistment.

His daughter, Grace, said the diary was used as a pillow to rest his head during long marches and encampments throughout Wyoming, Montana, South Dakota, North Dakota, and Nebraska. The actual page in the diary where a poem was located is in parentheses above each poem. A blank means the original diary script was not legible and could not be translated. The poems are reproduced as they appear in the diary, complete with misspellings and unusual punctuation and capitalizations.

(PAGE 1)
THE BETROTHAL

Over the barren plains
Two leisurely wind their way
As the _____ are well is closing
The muses of the day
O! Plainly tonight I see them
Though my tears fall thick and fast
As rises before my gazing
This memory of the past.

A narrow stream in their pathway
Calls for a sudden pause

When smiling as if in scorning
He lightly leaps across
Then reaching his hands to the maiden
Alone on the other side
He asks, "Will you trust me, darling
To help you over the tide?"

(Do you know that sometimes a motion,
A look or a careless word,
Reveals a fountain's waters
Now for the first time stirred?)

She pauses a moment trembling
  Then lays her palms on his own
One moment—and never after
  Can either be alone.

For turning each to the other
  Each looks in the other's eyes
This is their quiet betrothal
  But, it lasts for ever and aye
  But, it lasts for ever and aye

Poetry of my own Composition
is signed Moccasin Joe or M.J.

(PAGE 1 to 2)
MEMORY

Stand on a funeral mound
  Far, far from all that love thee:
With a barren heath around
  And a cypress tower above thee
And think awhile the sad wind frets
  And the night in cold gloom closes.
Of spring and spring's sweet violets
  Summer and summer's roses.

Sleep where the thunders fly
  Across the tossing billows
The canopy of sky.
  Wind, the lonely deck, the pillow;
And dream while the chill sea foam
  In mocking dashes o'er thee
Of the cheerful hearth, the quiet home
  And the kiss of her that loves thee.

Watch in the deepest cell
  Of the foreman's dungeon tower
Till hopes most cherished spell
  Has lost is cheering power

Talk of the minstrel lute
  Of the warrior's high endeavors
When the honeyed lips are muted
  And the strong arms cherished forever
Look back at the summer's sun

From the mist of dark December
Then say to the broken hearted one
  "Tis pleasant to remember."

(PAGES 3–4)
OVER THE DAM
by L. K. Bennet

(PAGE 4)
OUR HEROS SHALL LIVE
by Unknown Author

(PAGE 5)
PRINT TAYLOR'S EULOGY
by Wild Dan,
V&M *[Vermont & Massachusetts]* Railroad
known as Moccasin Joe

Print Taylor was the meanest man
  That ever saved a dime
He grudged the time it took to wash
  As though it were a crime.

When called upon the road to fix
  A cellar quick he dug
And when the men called loud for him
  He sold them Brandy from his jug.

For Print he had a little still
  Where brandy he did make
For all the money it brought him in
  Did soothe so many an ache.

Now Print sold part of his farm
  And just to make it last
He moved grapevines and apple trees
  Into the other part.

But Colton [Wm. A. Colton?] *said unto this man*
  Is this the way you do
If this is not quick settled up
  Why you, I'll quickly sue.

Now Print thought this was rather tough
  For when they met him upon the street

The neighbors always asked him
If he had not better treat.

Now Print had a very large family
Of children great and small
Oh! When they called the roll at night
He wondered if 'twas all.

(PAGE 6)

And midst the children gathering there
Was one who was oft called Booth
For he had shot a gay young girl
Now this is the very truth

Print he belonged to the pious sect
Where sin was never found
Yet still he played some poison tricks
When the parson wasn't round.

But when at last Hell gapes for him
He will go without any fuss
And this line shall be his Epitaph
"A miserable, ornery cuss."

(PAGE 6)
IN MEMORIUM
by Wild Dan, V&M RR, Moccasin Joe

Sweet spirit immortal to the skies now soar
When trials and sorrow shall trouble no more
You'll never more meet with us here below
But where you are we all may go
We know you are gone to the bright Heavenly home
Where those who love God will welcome may come
In that bright heavenly sphere you'll rejoice ever more
While all heaven ____ your are ____ ____ o'er.

(PAGE 7)
CLING TO THOSE WHO CLING TO YOU
by Unknown Author

(PAGES 8–9)
DRAFTED
by Unknown Author

(PAGE 9)
CONGRATULATIONS ON MARRIAGE DEDICATED TO MISS H. E. P. WEST JEFFERSON, OHIO
by Wild Dan, Moccasin Joe

On this joyful occasion
My best wishes I send
And sincerely hope the honey moon
May last till life shall end.

If you are mated as you are married
Then your life shall happy be
As you glide down the roll of years
To the long eternity.

That your life many be most happy
Is my most heartfelt prayer
And I hope and trust this loved one
Will shield you from all sorrow and care.

And when old age comes on
When your locks shall turn to grey
May the love you bear each other
Be as strong as it is today.

Though there's but friendship between us
Let's not lightly be it spoken
For I hope you will share the happiness
Of which your vow is taken.

(PAGE 10)
IN MEMORIAM
by Wild Dan, Moccasin Joe

She sleeps, She sleeps
Tread softly now
*   Never more we'll disturb her rest*
She is gone from our sight
to that far better Land
*   Ever more to dwell with the blest.*

She sleeps, She sleeps.
The spark of life has fled
*   And her sweet spirit is gone*
To her beautiful home in God's chosen land
*   Her Savior has called her home.*

She sleeps, She sleeps. Her earthly form
*   Here rests beneath the sod*
But her soul is gone to the mansions above
*   To dwell forever with God.*

She sleeps! She sleeps! We say she is dead.
*   Is free from all care and pain*
But she is only gone to her rest,
to her eternal home
*   Where saints immortal reign.*

Killed May 2nd at Greenfield, my roommate
J.J. Collins killed 20 minutes past 8 o'clock.

"In the midst of life we are in Death."

(PAGE 11)
THOUGHTS OF A SOLDIER
AFTER ENLISTING
by Wild Dan, Moccasin Joe

It was in Massachusetts
*   The city of Springfield*
That I joined the Regular Army
*   And was ready for the field.*

After I had enlisted
*   I loafed a pleasant week*
When one day in the office
*   I heard the Captain speak.*

I am from St. Louis
*   And there you must report*
For out upon the Border
*   Men are getting rather short.*

So we take the cars for Albany
*   A hundred miles away*
Expecting in that city
*   A day or two to stay.*

Now "Good-bye" friends and neighbors
*   With you I ne'er could rest*
So I'm bound to try my fortune
*   In the far distant West.*

At times I may be sorry
*   At others feel quite bad*
Yet such is my disposition
*   That I never shall be sad.*

So it's Good-bye friends and Kindred
*   We ne'er may meet again*
For perchance my bones may whiten
*   Mid the venture of the plains.*

(PAGE 12)
THINKING
by M.J.

I sit and think in the calm still night
 Of her who is gone from me.
And the thoughts lose themselves to foam
 Like the waves of some fierce sea

I think now of the hours that we so happily passed
 When the purity and innocence were all my own
Then comes the fearful darkness of the scene
 When they robbed my Darling for the tomb.

Oh! My beautiful Annie, my darling in Old Times
 My heart now feels the loneliness of life
But had you lived to cheer me as through the world we passed
 I ne'er should have been that lonely with you to cheer my life.

Yet God has chosen wisely for her the better part
 For me the cold deceitful world to tread
And learn his will upon this earth so vile
 Ere I too am numbered with the dead.

But when at last he calls us to meet in the world above
 And in that eternal life be united ever more
We will walk the flowery Kingdom and think of the days now gone
 Those happy hours we passed upon this earthly shore.

Till such a time as he calls me I faithful will be
 And try to make myself worthy of her love
And learn the lessons of Faith, Hope and Charity till the time
 "Come up higher" sounds from the throne above.

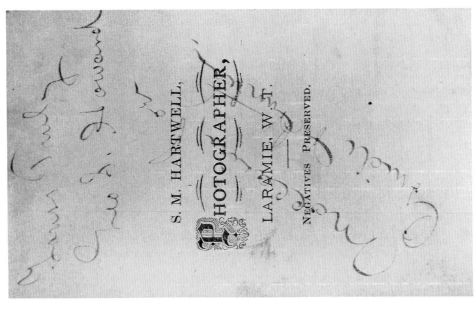

Photograph courtesy of Jack Strohm.

George S. Howard (top left) was photographed in his sergeant's fatigue jacket in Laramie City, Wyoming Territory. George signed the back (top right) of the photograph, "Yours Truly Geo. S. Howard Moccasin Joe—Guide and Hunter." Photographed by S. M. Hartwell.

(PAGE 13)
SCOUTING
by Scar Head the Crazy Scout,
Moccasin Joe

It's a lone, still night on the prairie
*   With the coyotes howling wild*
And the calm, clear sky is covering
*   A bold New England child.*

For there is trouble on the Border now
*   And we have left the Post*
And, blood may be the cost.

For in this border warfare
*   Full many a form is left*
To rot upon the prairie
*   Quick of its life bereft.*

For many a dusky warrior
*   Has learned right well the spot*
Where a soldier's life will leave him
*   Before a carbine shot.*

But we all must take our chances
*   In life's great battlefield*
Who will be the first to yield.

For death comes to us all
*   Although in different forms*
You may die 'mid friends
*   And I midst wars alarms*

But when our work is finished
*   And we are called to rest*
My sleep will be as peaceful
*   Neath the prairie of the West.*

(PAGE 14)
ON GUARD
by Scar Head the Crazy Scout,
Moccasin Joe

Sitting in the guard house
*   Waiting to wake my relief*
My thoughts take the form of poetry
*   But my story must be brief.*

Sitting thus I think
*   Of the girl I loved*
In that happy time
*   When the heart is easy moved.*

I thought she was well fitted
*   My life to happy make*
But, alas she played me false
*   When my name she agreed to take.*

But I cherish no anger now
*   For I may soon lay down*
The life that she has blighted
*   On some fierce Battle Ground.*

So farewell my darling Nellie
*   Although you used me wrong*
Yet the lesson that you taught me
*   Only made my life more strong.*

Tho come the gentler feelings
*   Of Mother and my Home*
And when my bondage is over
*   To you I'll surely come.*

I think now of the time
*   In my boyhood's bright days*
When my gentle, gentle Mother
*   Taught me better, holier ways.*

Then gay laughing days
*   Were closed by still night*
With holy prayers she led me
*   To God's great throne of white.*
Although I ne're may meet them
*   Who have caused me joy and pain*

Yet sometimes we'll be gathered
On the great judgment plain.

But time is passing onward
The guard I now must call
So farewell all my darlings
If on the field I fall.

FORGOTTEN

by Scar Head the Crazy Scout, Moccasin Joe

If I could only forget and be forgotten.

Out of sight and soon forgotten
'Tis a soldier's weary cry
Out of sight and soon forgotten
Friends will let my memory die. (no, never)*

You I cherished long and fondly
In the days now past and gone
But 'mid new friends you've forgotten
I must tread the path all alone.

May the new friends that you've found
Be true to you always
As true as is this soldier
On the Border far away.

Lone night as you await
The coming of a guest
Then let your thoughts a moment
Upon this soldier rest.

*[Comment by Carrie O'Patrick of Saratoga Precinct, Omaha, Nebraska. This note by Carrie is one of several she enters into the margins of George's diary. As I translated, I grew to recognize her handwriting and when I discovered her poem I was able to match the comments.]

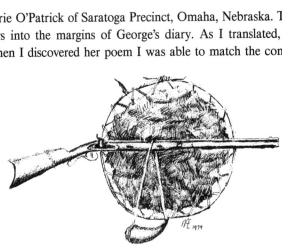

(PAGE 16)
Lines written on the Death of Lieut. Robinson who was killed by Indians Feb. 9th 1874 near Fort Laramie
by Moccasin Joe

[George was one of the men assigned to locate Lt. Robinson's body and bring it back to Fort Laramie for proper burial. He and a small group of scouts recovered the body shortly after Robinson and a corporal were killed.]

He is gone to his rest
    To his last long home
Where Drum-beat nor Roll-call
    Shall ever more come.

Where no dusky savage
    Rides his untamed steed
And friends are ever near
    In the hour of need.

He will have no more rides
    His life to save
In that Heavenly Post
    Beyond the grave.

In that beautiful Land
    There's neither trouble nor care
But each spirit is free
    And light as air.

In a Legion of Angels
    He will serve ever more
While we know that for him
    All troubles are o'er.

May your Life be as free from Sin as all the pages of this Book within.

(PAGE 17)
SCAR HEAD'S LOVE LETTER (is a good one)*
by Moccasin Joe, George Howard

Please excuse the abruptness
  *With which I you address (certainly)**
But still some few of my thoughts
  To you I will express

I have been sometime in the Army
  And have learned right well its ways
Yet it is hard to pass away the time
  These dull cold winter days.

And, to pass the long hour by
  *To you I thought I would write (just so)**
I'll try and say nothing improper
  And I hope you'll excuse it quite
      *(all right)**

*The Indians are full plenty (so?)**
  In the foothills 'mong the woods
They sometimes kill a citizen
  And then steal all his goods

I see a good deal of them
  For to the Cavalry I belong
And we always have to chase them
  *When they do anything wrong (strange!)**

And many a night on the prairie
  With the coyotes howling wild
The calm blue sky's been a covering
  A bold New England child
      *(sad, but 'tis true)**

The weather is quite pleasant
  In the neighborhood of the Post
But when the wind blows on the prairie
  *It's quite easy to get lost (How you talk!)**

* Comments by Carrie O'Patrick,
Saratoga Precinct, Omaha, Nebraska.

(PAGE 18)
Perchance you would like to know me
  At least my name find out
Well, in this part of the country
  I'm known as Scar Head the Crazy Scout

Now if you will answer
  This letter from the West
Then I will write another
  And set your mind at rest

But farewell for the present
  I've written a long letter
But if you will answer this
  I will write the next one better.

THE CURSE OF KEHAMA
by Unknown Author

(PAGE 19)
RETROSPECTION
by Moccasin Joe

On this dreary rainy night
  I sit in my tent alone
My thoughts are those of bitterness
  My music the sad winds moan
For each life has its grief
  Its sorrow and its woe
And no one can escape them
  While they tread the earth below.

I think this dreary night
  Of my old New England home
And the time when such thoughts as these
  To my breast ne'er dared to come
Then rainy nights were a pleasure
  And my sleep was the most sound
For I slept with a mother's blessing
  And a mother's prayer around.

But years have passed since then
    And I've traveled many a mile
But I never can forget those hours
    For memory helped them all the while.
And on that bright Spring morning
    Full many a year ago
When I left that home and loved ones
    To travel the wide world through.

The earth was decked in its brightest
    Calm and quiet all around
Each tree to its topmost branches
    With dark green leaflets crowned.
My heart had no thought of sorrow
    Of grief, care, nor pain
Oh! Those happy youthful hours
    That ne'er can come again.

(PAGE 20)
I found each life was a battle
    Each heart was a battle field
Where might would try to triumph
    And cause the Right to yield
And Satan and his demons
    Waged constant warfare there
'Gainst Christ and His good angels
    So beautiful and fair.

And who has won the battle
    I must leave for other tongues
For to keep the Tempter down
    I must fight 'till life is done
But I'll fight the battle bravely
    And try and do my best
'Till the wicked cease from troubling
    And the weary are at rest.

But, I think tonight of that home
    'Mid the green New England hills
Where life was a round of pleasure
    And I ne'er knew of its ills
Oh! That I might be there
    This rainy night so cold
T'would seem like youth again
    Although I'm growing old.

But it may not be my lot in life
    To look on those scenes once more
And recall the happy scenes
    That I saw from that cottage door
Yet 'till God calls me hence
    My memory will be bright
Of the youthful hours I passed
    Around that evening light.

(PAGES 21–23)
ON THE SHORES OF TENNESSEE
by E. L. Beebe

(PAGES 24–25)
ON TO FREEDOM
by Duganne

(PAGE 25–26)
THOSE MILLS OF GOD
by Unknown Author

NIGHT by Unknown Author

(PAGE 27)
IRONSIDES
by Unknown Author

(PAGES 28–29)
THE OCEAN BURIAL
by Unknown Author

(PAGE 30)
THE OLD SEXTON
by Unknown Author

(PAGE 31–32)
THE LABORER
by Unknown Author

(PAGES 32–33)
SELECTIONS FROM BOZZARIS
by Unknown Author

(PAGE 33)
NO SUBMISSION
by Unknown Author

(PAGES 34–35)
THERE'S BUT ONE PAIR OF STOCKINGS TO MEND TONIGHT
by Unknown Author

(PAGES 36–37)
BINGEN ON THE RHINE
by Unknown Author

(PAGE 37)
WORSHIP IN NATURE
by Bethune

(PAGES 38–40)
BARBARA FREITCHIE *[Frietchie]*
by J. G. Whittier

(PAGE 40)
MY MOTHER'S BIBLE
by Unknown Author

(PAGE 41)
SELF-RESPECT
by Unknown Author

(PAGES 42–43)
FARE THEE WELL
by Lord Byron

(PAGES 44–46)
THANATOPSIS
by William J. Bryant at the age of 18 years. Now 80 years old (1874).

(PAGES 46–47)
INDUSTRY
by William Leggett, N.A.R.

(PAGE 48)
THE GENIUS OF DEATH
by Unknown Author

(PAGES 49–55)
EXTRACT FROM ROBERT EMMET'S SPEECH

(PAGES 55–56)
TWILIGHT
by Unknown Author

(PAGES 57–58)
SENTIMENT OF 1812
by Unknown Author

(PAGE 59)
THE BIBLE
by Unknown Author

(PAGES 60–61)
SORROW FOR THE DEAD
by Unknown Author

Good Bye Old Book. No more we'll meet! (Yes. We will too. I'm happy to see you.)*
Comment by Carrie O'Patrick

(PAGES 62–64)
THE AMERICAN UNION
by Dan'l. Webster (July 1874.)

(PAGES 65–71)
THE RIDE OF COLLINS GRAVES
by Sidney Dickinson*
*A mighty poor poet, Sidney Dickinson, Amherst, Mass. Relative of Emily. *[This comment was written in the margin of the page by George.]*

(PAGES 72–74)
AN INCIDENT OF FLOOD MAY 16th, 1874 ON MILL RIVER
by Unknown Author

(PAGE 74)
WILL YOU COME TO MEET ME, DARLING? by Unknown Author

(PAGE 75)
GRADATION by Moccasin Joe

Heaven is not reached at a single bound.
But we build the ladder by which we rise.
From the lowly earth to the vaulted skies.

I count this thing to be grandly true
That a noble deed is a step toward God
Raising the soul from the common sod
To a purer air and broader view

When the morning calls us to light and life
But our heart's grow weary and e're the might
Our lives are trailing the sordid dust

We hope, we resolve, we aspire, we pray
And seem to mount the air on wings
Beyond the recall of sensual things
But our feet still cling to the heavy clay

Wings for angels feet—for men
We may borrow the wings to find the way
We may hope resolve aspire and pray
But our feet must rise or we fall again

Only in dreams is a ladder thrown
From the weary earth to the sapphire walls
But the dream departs the vision falls
And the sleeper wakes on his pillow of stone

Heaven is not reached at a single bound
We build the ladder by which we rise
From the lowly earth to the vaulted skies
And mount to its summit round by round

(A sermon in few words by Moccasin Joe, G.H.)

(PAGES 76–77)
THE RESOLUTE MOTHER
by Mrs. Hemars

(PAGE 77)
FOR YOU
by Hesta Benedict

(PAGES 78–79)
BIJOU
by Unknown Author

(PAGE 79)
MEMORY
by Unknown Author

(PAGE 80)
I DO NOT DRINK, DEAR MOTHER
by George Howard, Moccasin Joe
    (I do – Carrie O'Patrick)
[Comment by Carrie O'Patrick, frequent companion to Moccasin Joe when he was stationed in Omaha Barracks, Nebraska.]

Dear Mother, I got your letter
    Oh, how it cheered my heart
So far away from home and friends
    Doing the workers part
You ask about my habits
    Pray, set your mind at rest
I do not drink dear mother
    And I try to do my best.

The tempters they are many.
    The tempted they are more.
And they often sail in their painted ships
    Quite smoothly from the shore
But in looking down the river
    (Their sufferings, who can tell)
I see the struggling, helpless forms
    I see the wrecks as well.

I see on shore friends weeping
    I hear their children cry
And again I see the cruel waves
    Still running mountain high
I stretch my hand to save them
    Above the breakers roar

Too late! Too late! in sight of home
They sink to rise no more.

I will not drink dear mother
and I'll try to do my best
(God helping me) while absent.
So set your heart at rest
Oh! Happy, happy mother
A victory you have won
And you, the loving heart have blessed
Oh! happy thoughts, a son.

(PAGE 81)
IN MEMORIAM by Geo. Howard

Oh summer sky so blue and clear
O sparkling eyes without a tear
And joyous hearts without a fear

Oh earth so sweet and roses fair
And bright birds glistening through the air
Trilling soft music everywhere

A form I loved so true and well
Naught on this earth can break the spell
That links me to thy narrow cell

Where lies thy quiet peaceful breast
In childhood's hours I've oft caressed
Those loving lips I've often pressed

Oh! life is sweet when love is young
To cheer us as we urge along
This toilsome path, this busy throng

I think of thee at morning light
I see thee in my dreams by night
Thou art my guardian angel bright

I'll love thee still while life shall last
Nor fame, nor fortune, e'er can blast
Thy radiance o'er my memory cast.

(PAGES 82–83)
AT THE DOORS OF THE YEARS
by Unknown Author

(PAGE 83)
THE SEA
by Dana

(PAGE 84)
A PLEA FOR REST
by Geo. S. Howard, Moccasin Joe

But one boon my heart desires.
I have walked among the briars
Oh so long my feet have failed me
Sorrow has so long assailed me
Having naught of love to find me
I would leave it all behind me
Tired and o so sore distressed
This my plea—Lord give me rest
Sweet rest!

Tired I am of care and sorrow
Tired of waiting for the morrow
That shall come to me—never!
I would leave it all forever
Leave earth's turmoil and its riot
For the still and endless quiet
Where within the human breast
Comes no wailing plea for rest—
Sweet rest

Earth o mother in compassion
Flowery pillows for my fashion
Broider it with fern and daises
That I sleeping in their mazes
Neath the roses and the clover
Ne'er a sad dream shall dream over
Pain so long has me oppressed
Grant my simple prayer for rest
Sweet rest!

(PAGES 85–86)
WHAT HAVE YOU DONE?
by Unknown Author

(PAGE 87)
THE LOOM OF LIFE
by Unknown Author

> *Weary of living so weary!*
> *Longing to lie down and die*
> *To find for the sad heart and dreary*
> *The end of the pilgrimage nigh.*
>
> *Weary so weary of wishing*
> *For a form that is gone from my sight*
> *For a voice that is hushed to me ever*
> *For eyes that to me were so bright.*
>
> *For a hand to land on my forehead*
> *A glimpse of the golden brown hair:*
> *For a step that to me was sweet music*
> *And a brow that was noble and fair.*
>
> *Weary so weary of waiting!*
> *Waiting for sympathy sweet:*
> *For something to love and to love me*
> *And pleasures that are not fleet.*
>
> *Tired so tired of drifting*
> *Adorn the dark stream of life!*
> *Tired of treading the billows*
> *The billows of toil and strife!*
>
> *Wishing and wailing so sadly*
> *For love that was sweetest and best*
> *Willing to die O so gladly*
> *If that would bring quiet and rest.*
>
> *Moccasin Joe (Wild Dan)*

(PAGE 98)
THE LOVER'S PLEA
by Moccasin Joe

Love me, My Darling
*   With a strong love*
Like that we receive
*   From Heaven above.*

With a love that shall last
*   Through this vale of tears*
Grow stronger and better
*   Through the fast fleeting years.*

that shall help me so well
*   Life's burdens to bear*
Make light my sorrows
*   And pleasant my care.*

It shall help me so well
*   Breast Life's flowing stream*
So the long years to come
*   Shall pass like a dream.*

Then love me my darling
*   For I love you so well*
That I long in your presence
*   Forever to dwell.*

To help share your burdens
*   Your sorrow, your care*
Help you to be happy
*   And ne'er know despair.*

And when trials are over
*   And Life's journey done*
May we still be together
*   In our immortal home.*

(PAGE 99)
GOODBYE
by Moccasin Joe, Laramie, Wyo.

I wish you might be my Darling
*   For I've loved you so fondly, so well*
I have dreamed so oft of the happiness
*   When I in your presence should dwell.*

But no more must I be dreaming
*   For you care nothing for me*
No more than as though my existence
*   Was a wave of some far away sea*

You care not whether my burdens
*   Are easy or hard to bear*
Whether the life I am leading
*   Is filled with pleasure or care*

So farewell if down life's dark valley
*   I must lonely and weary plod on*
You may laugh perchance at my folly
*   When I to my grave have gone.*

Yet remember that on this broad earth
*   Most hearts have plenty of pain*
So please when you have other lovers
*   Don't repeat the sad tale again.*

Don't laugh about my folly
*   My wickedness, my sin*
But pray when death releases me
*   God's Heaven I may enter in.*

MIKE 78
5/21/78

(PAGE 100)
PRAY FOR ME, DARLING
(I will)* by Moccasin Joe

Oh Darling will you sometimes
    As your prayers ascend on high
Ask God to send a blessing
    To such a wretch as I.

Plead with Him so earnestly
    To grant that saving grace
That when my work is finished
    I may meet Him face to face.

That I may be one of his chosen
    Upon this earth below
So when Death calls me hence
    I may to his kingdom go.

That I may learn to know and love Him
    Who died on Calvary's tree
To open the gates of Heaven
    To poor sinners like me.

O ask Him in your prayers
    To show me my wickedness
That I may help some other
    His name to know and bless.

*[Comment by Carrie O'Patrick]

DARLING, DON'T YOU KNOW?
by Unknown Author

(PAGE 101)
MEMORIES
by T. H. Gilbert, Waverly Magazine.

FOR THEE AND ME
by Unknown Author

(PAGE 102)
WORKING MEN
by Unknown Author

SWEET PEACE
by Unknown Author by Ewoh,
from Waverly Magazine.

(PAGE 103)
THERE IS NO DEATH
from Waverly Magazine

(PAGE 104)
Sept. 7th 1874, Capt. Wells
[This date and the name of George's command-ing officer were written in the margin of the diary on page 104.]

I CANNOT WRITE TONIGHT
by Cassandra A. Thorndike

EVERY INCH A MAN
by James McCarroll

(PAGE 105)
WHY SHOULD WE STRIVE
by Mrs. Helen Hamlet
from Waverly Magazine.

(PAGE 106)
A MAGDALENS DEATH*
Found in stateroom of a young and beautiful woman who jumped overboard from a Fall River boat in '70 or '71. (Have pity on them for they're not entirely to blame.) [This note beside the poem was written by George.]

(PAGE 107)
MEMORIES
by Unknown Author

(PAGE 108)
A PLAINT
by Unknown Author

[The following passage is written in the margins of the diary on page 108.]

Fort Sanders, Wyoming, Feb. 20th 1877

    I do not know what makes me feel so bad tonight but I would like to be Home for a little while. Well I hope this winter may learn me something that I won't forget for awhile. Oh! I am so tired of living. Moccasin Joe is a soldier who served 5 years in "E" 2nd Cav. following Gen'l Crook all through the Campaign of 1876, living on horsemeat for 8 days.

(PAGE 109)
A BEAUTIFUL LAND
by Jennie Lawrence

(PAGE 110)
BEAR YOUR BURDENS!
by Hulda

(PAGES 110–112)
LORAINE
by Unknown Author

(PAGE 113–114)
JUNE
by William Cullen Bryant

(PAGE 114–115)
IN THE VALLEY
by Cora Neil Cody

(PAGE 116)
HERE LET ME REST
by J.E. Gray

(PAGE 117)
LONELY
by Joseph Redman Drake

(PAGE 118–119)
GUESTS OF THE HEART
by Unknown Author

(PAGE 119)
THERE REMAINETH AT REST
by Unknown Author

BEAUTY'S MAGIC
by Unknown Author

(PAGE 120)
TIRED
by Moccasin Joe,
Fort Laramie, September 1874.

Dear Mother, I am so weary
    So tired of sin and strife
Tired of wandering aimless
    For such has been my life
I would gladly go to my grave
    And sleep in the cold, cold gloom
For I know that rest and quiet
    Are found within the tomb.

I have been so tired and weary
    For the numberless long years
For my life is a round of trouble
    Beset by cares and fears
I would leave all this sorrow
    This pain, trouble and care
And sleep the last long sleep
    Find rest and quiet there.

My life has been so lonely
    With no one to cherish or love
And I cannot find the pathway
    That leads to God above (try, try again!)*
I would gladly leave the life
    And lie down with the dead
Where I would not heed the jar
    When gay feet should o'er me tread.

O Mother Earth in compassion
    Take me with in thy breast
For there beneath the flowers
    I may at least find rest
For within the silent grave
    No said spirit dares to come
Sorrow ne'er invades the portals
    Of the silent shadowy tomb.

*[Comment by Carrie O'Patrick]

THE SABBATH OF YOUTH
by Moccasin Joe, Sept 1874

I often think of the sabbath
Of my boyhood's golden time
And the sweetly tolling church bells
Of that far away Eastern chime

Oh the bells of the little church
That chimed so sweet in youth
Calling us from worldly thoughts
To hear and heed the truth.

O those pure, quiet sabbaths
Those holy days of rest
They seem today like stepping stones
To that land where dwell the blest

How little we heed in childhood
These blessed words of truth
"Remember now thy Creator
In these the days of thy youth."

O for one blessed sabbath
Like those holy days of old
Ere my feet began their wanderings
In search of the tempting gold

Could some kind and gentle fairy
Take me back as I used to be
With my knowledge of pain and sorrow
T'would seem like Heaven to me.

(PAGE 139)
FOOTSTEPS OF ANGELS
by Henry Wadsworth Longfellow

Omaha Barracks, Neb
Oct 27, '74

J. V. McCoy
Omaha Commercial College and
Miss Moore

[Signatures of two women were written in the margin. J. V. McCoy wrote a poem that appears in the diary.]

(PAGE 141–144)
PAUL REVERE'S RIDE
by Henry Wadsworth Longfellow

(PAGE 144)
SPEAK NO ILL
by Unknown Author

(PAGE 145)
AN ENGAGEMENT: ONLY A BROKEN VOW! WHAT THEN
by Unknown Author

(PAGE 146)
SOME ONE TO LOVE
by Unknown Author

WHAT IS LOVE?
by Unknown Author

VIGIL
by Unknown Author

(PAGE 147–148)
AT THE ALTAR
by Eben E. Rexford

Life before me looks dark and gloomy down to the wedding of the Dead where I shall meet my Annie of the quaint old Indian town.

[This sentence was written in the margin of page 148 by George.]

(PAGE 149)
HAVE COURAGE, MY BOY, TO SAY NO

Your starting on life's journey, my darling
Alone on the highway of life
You'll meet with a thousand temptations
Each city with evil is ripe
This world is a stage of excitement
There is danger wherever you go
But if you are tempted in weakness
Have courage, my boy, to say NO.

the sirens sweet song may allure you
Beware of he cunning and art
Whenever you see her approaching
Be guarded and haste to depart
The billiard saloons are inviting
Decked out in their tinsel and show
You may be invited to enter
Have courage, my boy, to say NO.

The bright ruby wine may be offered
No matter how tempting it be
From poison that strings like an adder
Have courage my boy to flee
The gambling halls are before you
Their lights, how they dance to and fro
If you should be tempted to enter
Think twice, even thrice, 'ere you go.

In courage alone lies your safety
I pray you'll try hard to win
And trust in your Heavenly Father
Who will keep you unspotted from sin
Temptations will go on increasing
As streams from a river let flow
But if you are true to your manhood
Have courage, my boy, to say NO.

Moccasin Joe for "Mother"

(PAGE 150)
MOTHER, IS THE OLD HOME LONELY?

Mother, is the old home lonely
With no children left, you there?
With no voices ringing gaily
And none hushed in solemn prayer?
Do you miss our thousand questions
That were asked in wild delight?
And our tramping up the stairway
After bidding you Good Night—

Mother, is the old home lonely
When you realize the fact
That Old Time with all his changes
Will not bring your children back?
Do you in your idle moments
Now your boys are grown up me!
Ask yourself that solemn question
Are they happy now as then

I will answer you that question
In a simple, careless way
That as men we live to labor
When as boys we lived to play
So it is while older growing
Joys and pleasures are but few
Those our recollections cherish
Passed when boys at Home with you.

(PAGE 151)
A STERLING OLD POEM

Who shall judge man from his manners?
Who shall know him by his dress?
Pampers may be fit for princes
Princes fit for something less
Crumpled shirt and dirty jacket
May beclothe the golden ore.
Of the deepest thoughts and feelings
Satin vest can do no more.

There are streams of crystal nectar
Ever flowing out of stone;
Where are purple beds and golden
Hidden crushed and over-thrown
God who counts by souls not dresses
Loves and prospers you and me
While he values thrones the highest
But as pebbles in the sea

Man appraised above his fellows
Oft forgets his fellows then
Masters, rulers, lords, remember
That your meanest hinds are men
Men of labor, men of feeling
Men of thoughts and men of fame
Claiming equal rights to sunshine
In man's ennobling name.

There are foam-embroidered oceans
There are little wood clad rills.
There are feeble inch-high saplings
There are cedars on the hills
God, who counts by souls not stations
Loves and prospers you and me
For to Him all vain distinctions
Are as pebbles in the sea.

Is a soldier worse for being in the Army than he was as a citizen when he lives an honest upright life before God and man?

M. J. (Moccasin Joe)

[George's comment is written in the margin beside the poem he wrote on pages 151 and 152.]

(PAGE 152)

Toiling hands alone are builders
      Of a nations wealth and fame
Titted laziness is pensioned
      Fed and fattened on the same
By the seat of other foreheads
      Living only to rejoice
While the poor man's out-raged freedom
      Vainly lifts its feeble voice

Truth and justice are eternal
      Born with loveliness and light
Secret wrongs shall never prosper
      While there is a sunny right
God, whose words-wide voice is singing
      Boundless love to you and me
Links oppressions with its titles
      But as bubbles in the sea.

FOR PEOPLE WITHOUT CHILDREN

Could heartlessness be more
Or meanness well be meaner
Read the advertisement below
From Monday morning Gleaner
"A stately residence to let
With all conveniences complete
      "For people without children."

Who e're the cruel sentence wrote
Has outraged Christ's injunction
Suffer them and forbid them not
Doubtless with son all compunction
Go tell the wicked man in sooth
How cold his words—nay how uncouth.
      "For people without children."

(Page 153)

He pats his dog and pets his cat
For them he has causes;
But children must not cross his mat
The best of pets he misses
How blithe is life 'ere youth is gone

And yet how desolate how lone
      "For people without children."

Half wasted were the many joys
Which Heaven upon us showers
If twere not for our girls and boys
Our sprigs and buds and flowers.
Such thoughts I ween may not come nigh
To those who have a single eye
      "For people without children."

Your next advertisement may date
From more contracted quarters
Four low, dank walls with narrow gate
Which opens on Lethis waters
'Ere then improve the time in store
Relent and open wide your door
      "To people who have children."

(PAGE 154

OVER THE HILL TO THE POOR HOUSE

Over the hill to the poor-house I'm trudgin my weary way
I a woman of seventy, and only a trifle gray
I who am smart an chipper, for all the years I've told
As many another woman that's only half as old.

Over the hill to the poor-house. I can't quite make it clear!
Over the hill to the poor-house it seems so horrid queer!
Many a step I've taken a-toilin' to and fro
But this is a sort of journey I never thought to go.

What's the use of heapin' on me a pauper's shame
Am I lazy or crazy? Am I blind or lame?
I'm not so supple, nor yet so awful stout.
But charity ain't no favor, if one can live without!

I am willin' and anxious an' ready any day
To work for a decent livin' an' pay my honest way
For I can earn my victuals an' more too I'll be bound.
If anybody only is within to have me around.

Once I was young and han'some, I was upon my soul
Once my cheeks was roses, my eyes as black as coals;
And I can't remember in them days of hearin' people say
For any kind of reason that I was in their way.

Taint no use of boasting or talkin over free—
But many a house an' home was open then to me
Many a han'some offer I had too from likely men
An' nobody ever hinted that I was a burden then

And when John an' I was married sure he was good an' smart
But he an' all the neighbors would own, I done my part.
For life was all before, me an' I was young an' strong
I worked the best I could in tryin' to get along.

(PAGE 155)

And so we worked together and life was hard but gay.
With now and then a baby to cheer us on our way:
Till we had half a dozen an' all growed clean an' neat
An' went to school like others an' had enough to eat.

So we worked for the children an' raised em' every one
Worked for 'em summer an' winter gusts -as we right to've done
Only perhaps we humored 'em which some good folks condems
But every couple's childr'ns a heap the best to them.

Strange how much we think of our blessed little ones
I'd have died for my daughters! I'd have died for my sons
And God he made the rule of love: but when we're old and gray
I've noticed it sometimes home how fails to work the other way.

Strange another thing: when our boys an' girls was grown
And when exception' Charley they'd left us there alone
When John he nearer an hearer come an' dearer seemed to be
The Lord of Hosts He came one day an' took him away from me.

Still I was bound to struggled an' never to cringe or fall
Still I worked for Charlie for Charley was now my all
And Charley was pretty good to me with scarce a word or frown
Till at last he went a courtin' an' brought a wife from town.

She had an' education an' that was good for her.
But when she twitted me on mine 'twas carryin' things to fur
An I told her once 'fore company (an' it almost made her sick)
That I never swallowed a grammar or 'el a'rithmetic.

So 'twas only few days before the thing was done
They was a family of themselves an' I another one:
And a very little cottage one family will do.
But I never have seen a house that was big enough for two

An' I never could speak to suit her never could please her eye
An' it made me independent an' then I didn't try
But I was terrible staggered an' fell it like a blow
When Charley turned again me an' told me I must go.

(PAGE 156)

I went to live with Susan but Susan 's house was small
An' she was always hintin' how smug it was for us all.
An' what with her husband's sisters an' what with her children three
'Twas easy to discover that there wasn't roam for me.

An' then I went to Thomas the oldest son I've got
For Thomas' buildings'd cover the half an ache lot:
But all the childs'n was on me I couldn't stand their sauce
And Thomas said I needn't think I was comin' there to boss

An' then I wrote to Rebecca, my girl, that lives out West
An' to Isaac not far from her, some twenty miles at best
An' one of them said twas to warm there for anyone so old
An' t'other had an opinion the climate was to cold.

So they shirked an' slighted me an' shifted me about.
So they have well nigh soured me, an' wore my old heart out
But still I've born it pretty well an' wasn't much put down
Till Charley went to the poor master an' put me on the town

Over the hill to the poor house my children dear, good-bye,
Many a night I've watched you when only God was nigh
An' God'll judge between us: but I will always pray.
That you shall never suffer the half I do today.

[George Howard died in a poorhouse in 1887 after being shot through the neck. It is ironic that he wrote a poem in 1874 about the poorhouse more than ten years before his death.]

(Page 157)
CURFEW MUST NOT RING TONIGHT

Slowly England's sun was setting o'er the hilltops far away.
Filling all the land with beauty at the close of one sad day.
And the last rays kissed the forehead of a man and maiden fair.
He with footsteps slow and weary she with sunny floating hair
He with bowed head, sad and thoughtful, she with lips cold and white
Struggled to keep back a murmur—Curfew must not ring tonight.

"Sexton," Bessie's while lips faltered pointing to the person old.
With its turrets tall and gloomy with its walls dark, damp and cold
"I've a lover in that prison, doomed this very night to die
At the ringing of the Curfew and no other help is nigh:
Cromwell will not come till sunset—" and her lyres grew strangely
As she breathed the husky whisper—"Curfew must not ring tonight."

Bessie calmly spoke the sexton every word pierced her heart
Like the piercing of an arrow, like a deadly poisoned dart
Long, long years I've rung the Curfew from that gloomy shadowed tower
Every evening just at sunset it has told the twilight hour
I have done my duty ever tried to do it just and right
Now I'm old I still must do it—Curfew it must ring tonight.

Wild her eyes and pale her features stern and white, her thoughtful brow
And within her secret bosom Bessie made a solemn vow.
She had listened while the judges read with out a tear or sigh
At the ringing of the Curfew. Basil Underwood must die
And her breath came fast and faster and her eye grew large and
    bright
In an undertone she murmured—"Curfew must not ring tonight."

She with quick steps bounded forward spring within the old
  church tower
Left the old man threading slowly paths so oft he'd trod before
Not one moment paused the maiden but with eye and cheek aglow
Mounted up the gloomy tower where the bell swung to and fro
And she climbed the ladder on which fell no ray of light
Up and up—her white lips saying—Curfew must not sing tonight

She has reached the topmost ladder o'er her hangs the great dark bell
Awful is the gloom beneath her like a pathway down to hill
Lo the ponderous tongue is swinging 'tis the hour of Curfew now
And the sight has chilled her bosom stopped her breath and paled
  her brow
Shall she let it ring? No, never! Flash her eyes with sudden light
And she springs and grasps it firmly Curfew must not sing tonight

Out she swung far out the city seemed a speck of light below
Twixt heaven and earth her form suspended as the bell swing to and fro
And the sexton at the bell rope old and deaf heard not the bell
But he thought it still was ringing for young Basils funeral
  knell,
Still the maiden clung most firmly and with trembling lips and
  white
Said to hush her heart's wild beating Curfew must not ring
  tonight.

It was o'er the bell ceased swaying and the maiden stepped over more
Firmly on the dark old ladder where for hundred years before
Human foot had not been planted. The brave deed that she had done
Would be told long ages after, as the rays of setting sun
Should illume the sky with beauty: aged sires with heads of white
Long should tell the little children Curfew did not ring that
  night

O'er the distant hills came Cromwell, Bessie sees him and her brow
Full of hope and full of gladness, has no anxious traces now.
At her feet she tells her story shows her hands all bruised and
  torn
And her face so sweet and pleading yet with sorrow pale and worn
Touched her heart with sudden pity let his eyes with misty light
"Go! Your lover lives," said Cromwell, "Curfew shall not sing tonight."

This book has been the companion of a soldier for five years but now he bids it good-bye.

Yours, Moccasin Joe

(PAGE 159)
FROM DARKNESS TO LIGHT

Sorrow her pall had hung o'er me.
With no sunlight to brighten the gloom;
And the young life that should have been
so bright
Was wishing for rest in the tomb

My life had been filled with trouble
For so many long weary year
And each turn of the "Wheel of fortune"
Only brought new cares and fears

The light had long been hidden
The sunshine was dark as the night
'Till one day among the wild flowers
I found a Daisy that brought sweet light

That Daisy at last consented
With me to my life's stormy stream
And try and make the years to come
Pass happily by like a dream

The light that Daisy brought to me
Seemed sent from that Heaven above
Where dwell the beautiful Angels
And a God whose name is Love

Life no more to me seems dreary
The clouds hang no more like a pall
Her love has dispelled the gloom
And the bright sun now shines over all

And to you who of Life are a weary
Find a flower like this full of light
Whose presence through Life's dark battles
Will dispel all the gloom of the night—

Moccasin Joe

(PAGE 160)
THE WANDERERS RETURN

Good morning, Sir; yes, 'tis a beautiful day.
Walk in, Sir, and take a chair;
You look weary and worn;
traveled far, did you say?
Ah, I thought you'd a foreign air!

I've a lad, somewhere in foreign parts;
Perhaps you have met him? You smile!
Oh, Ned! it is you, deep down in my heart
I have felt it all the while.

No wonder I dared not call your name!
You're bearded, brown and tall;
While the boy who left me ten years since,
Was beardless, fair and small,
Alone, am I? Yes! They are scattered all.
Some to other homes; some to the grave.
You glance at your Father's vacant chair:
He sleeps 'neath the ocean wave.

And Susie? She's married and gone out West:
She married your old chum, Joe:
And a brave manly fellow he is, dear Ned.
Though a wild boy he was, you as you know.
And John? He's a merchant and lives in New York:
Getting rich there too, they say:
But the struggle for gold has changed him much:
Already his locks are grey.

George S. Howard

And Lucy! She sleeps on your sunny slope
Where as children together you've played.
She lived to see her every hope
Of happiness wither and fade
We could not mourn when we saw her go;
She said, "Death to me means rest!"
Bury me there in my favorite spot
And plant roses above my breast.

(PAGE 161)

And Ellie? She was ever your pet, I know.
She has gone: drifted away.
Dead? Ah, no: it were better so!
Not dead, but gone astray.
You weep. Would that I could weep such tears:
'Twould ease this burning pain
That has gnawed at my heart since that bitter day
When I knew of poor Ellie's shame.

There's another of whom you would hear, I see;
I can read your eager eyes.
She's living near us single, still.
Though many have sought the prizes.
And as you, dear Ned, do you come heart free?
Has your life been pure and free?
Can you ask her to place her hand in yours,
And tread life's path with thee?
Then go her heart has long been yours.
And with woman's love and faith
She need look but once in those clear blue eyes
To see that her heart is safe.
He's gone without even a cup of tea.
Oh, why did I chatter so!
But I'll sit the table with plates for three;
She'll come back with him soon, I know.

Run, Hannah, and light the kitchen fire!
Make the biscuit—spare not the cream;
While I bring from the cellar the raspberry jam.
Oh dear! it seems like a dream?
There's the frosted cake in the jar upstairs:
And the custard pie, yellow as gold.
I never baked one but I thought of him:
'Twas his favorite dainty of old.

(PAGE 162)

How bright is the world since yesterday!
How brilliant the robins song!
How heavy the air with fragrance
From the apple blossoms thrown!
Ah! life is sweet and God is good!
I will doubt him never more,
Hark! I hear the click of the garden gate
I will meet them at the door
They are come and with them a drooping form,
Clad in sables of deepest woe.
'Tis Ellie, my daughter, returned at last!
Now, indeed, doth my cap o'er flow!

The best handwriting of Moccasin Joe

THE DEAD SUMMER

Gone is the fair young Spring-time
with the fresh green leaves on her brow
And the sick perfume of her hawthorn bloom
Is but a memory now
Over loved the voice of her song-birds,
And the light of her velvet-eyes!
But she passed away with the hours of May
As a strain of music dies
And I think we should have mourned her
But before our eyes were wet
Came a fairer face and a statelier grace
To banish our regret

For the beautiful rose-wreathed Summer
Was filling the earth with bloom
So the primrose died by the river side
And no tear drops marked its tomb
O sweet was the light of her dawning
And the hush of her dusky eyes
When the star beams danced on the waves
that glanced
To the earth of alder leaves

(PAGE 163)

And her gifts were so much greater
Than the gifts of Spring had been
That we bent at the feet of this lady sweet
And owned her our sovereign queen

We roamed by her side through the meadows
*   She led us where great tress grew*
I arching bowers o'er brakes of flowers
*   All glimmering gold and blue—*
Where the wild rose nodded in fragrance
*   And the woodbine gleamed like snow—*
And the broom hung flakes of bloom
*   O'er the crag and valley low—*
Till our hearts bowed down to the Giver
*   And thrilled with a warmer glow*
For the joys that lay on our pilgrim way
*   As flowers by the wayside grow*

But a change came over her beauty
*   The while we rejoiced in its light*
Still as evening dies in the Western skies
*   E'en so did she pass from our sight*
And already O beautiful Summer
*   We long for thy coming again*
As we hear the wail of the Autumn gale
*   And the beat of the Autumn rain*
But the joy that endureth forever
*   Unsullied by change or gloom*
Is kept in love by our Father's above
*   Till we wake from our sleep in the tomb.*

(PAGE 164–165)
OUR TRUNDLE BED
Poem by J. V. McCoy, difficult to transcribe.

(PAGE 166)
THE BRIDGE OF SIGHS

One more unfortunate,
Weary of breath,
Rashly important,
Gone to her death!

Take her up tenderly,
Lift her with care;
Fashioned so slenderly,
Young and so fair!

Look at her garments
Clinging like cerements;
Whilst the wave constantly
Drips from her clothing
Take her up instantly
Loving not loathing.

Touch her not scornfully:
Think of her mournfully.
Gentle and humanly;
Not of the stains of her,
All that remains of her
Now , is pure womanly.

Make no deep scrutiny
Into her mutiny
Rash and undutiful;
Past all dishonor
Death has left on her
Only the beautiful.

Still for all slips of hers.
One of her family
Wipe those poor lips of hers
Oozing so calamity.

(PAGE 167)
Loop up her tresses
Escaped from the comb
Her fair auburn tresses;
Whitst wonderment guesses
Where was her home!

Who was her father?
Who was her mother?
Had she a sister?
Had she a brother?
Or was there a dearer one
Still and a nearer one
Yet, than all other.

Alas! for the rarity
Of Christian charity
Under the sun!
Oh! it was pitiful!
Near a whole city full.
Home she had gone.

Sisterly, brotherly,
Fatherly, motherly,
Feelings had changed;
Love, by harsh evidence,
Thrown from its eminence;
Even God's providence
Seeming estranged.

Where the lamps quiver
So far in the river
With many a light
From window and casement
From garret to basement
She stood with amazement
Horseless by night,

The bleak winds of March
Made her tremble and shiver

(PAGE 168)
But not the dark arch
Of the black flowing river:
Mad from life's history,
Glad to death's mystery,
Swift to be hurled
Anywhere anywhere
Out of the world!

In she plunged boldly
No matter how coldly
The rough river ran
Picture it—think of it,
Dissolute Man!
Love in it, drink in it
Then, if you can!

Take her up tenderly,
Lift her with care;
Fashioned so slenderly,
Young and so fair!

Ere her limbs frigidly
Stiffen to rigidly
Decently, kindly
Smooth and compose them;
And her eyes close them
Staring so blindly
Dreadfully staring
Through muddy impurity
As when with the daring
Last look of despairing
Fixed on purity,
             Over her breast!

Perishing, gloomily
Sparred by consumely.
Cold inhumanity,
Burning insanity.
Into her rest,
Cross her hand humbly
As if praying dumbly.
Owning her weakness
Her evil behavior.
And leaving with meekness,
Her sins to her Savior.

(PAGE 169)
APOSTROPHE TO LIVE BY

Once more I breathe the mountain air: once more
I tread my own free hills! My lofty soul
Throws all its fetters off: In its proud flight,
'Tis like the new fledged eaglet, whose strong wing
Soars to the sun it long has gazed upon
With eye undazzled. O! ye mighty race
That stand like frowning giants: fixed to guard
My own proud land: why did ye not hail down
The thundering avalanche when at your feet
The base usurper stood? A touch, a breath,
Nay, even the breath of prayer, ere now, has brought
Destruction on the hunter's head: and yet,
The tyrant passed in safety: God of Heaven!
Where slept thy thunder rolls?

Oh! with what pride I used
To walk these hills and look up to my God!
This land was vice.
From end to end, from cliff to take t'was free.
Free as our torrents are, that leap our rocks,
And plow our valleys;
So as our peaks that wear their caps of snow
In very presence of the regal sun!
How happy was I in it—then loved
Yes, I have sat and eyed
The thunder breaking from his cloud and smiled
To see him shake his lightnings o'er my head
And think I had no master save his own.

Liberty!

Thou choices, a gift of Heaven and wanting which
Life is as nothing. Hast thou then forgot
Thy native home? Must the feet of slaves
Pollute this glorious scene? It can not be!
Even as the smile of Heaven can pierce the depths
Of these dark caves and bid the wild flowers bloom
In spots where man has never dared to tread:
So thy sweet influence still is seen amid
These breathing cliffs. Some hearts still beat for thee.
And bow alone to Heaven. Thy spirit lives.

Ay, and shall live, when even the very names
Of tyrants is forgot.

Lo! while I gaze
Upon the mist that wreathes yon mountains brow.
The sunbeam touches it—and it becomes
A crown of glory on its hoary head,
O! is not this a passage of the dawn
Of freedom o'er the world? Hear me, then, bright
And beaming Heaven! while kneeling thus I vow
To live for Freedom or with her to die!

THE BOW
by Mrs. Hermans

(PAGE 172–173)
THE DEATH FIRE
by Mrs. Stephens

(Copied by Moccasin Joe)

Geo. Howard
Hinsdale, N. Hampshire

PAGES 174 TO 177
poem by William Cullen Bryant,
copied by George Howard.

PAGE 178 AND HALF OF 179
THE INDIAN WOMAN
by Mrs. Hermans.

(PAGE 178)
NO MORE or THE CAVALRY SOLDIER'S FAREWELL
Moccasin Joe

No more for me the bullets song
No more those rides that seem so long
No more the ground shall be my bed
No more on Bacon I'll be fed

No more to use before the Sun
No more on Guard when night is come
No more to bed and hunger feel
No more be hunting a square meal

No more in the soup I live for a bean
No more fat pork without some ham
No more to water call or stable
No more to groom as long as able

No more to fight Bad Faces' band
No more to hunt them from the land
No more be roaming o'er the Plains
No more be guarding wagon trains

My time is out, I'm going Home
I wish to God I'd never come
Out here to sleep in Rain and Snow
No more for thirteen dollars I know.

[George earned $13 per month which is why he mentions this amount in the poem.]

(PAGE 180–182)
THE ABORIGINES OF AMERICA
by Mrs. Sigourney

Copied by the poor Penman and crazy galoot, Geo. Howard of Co. E, 2nd Cavalry, Omaha Barracks, Nebraska, USA

Nothing but Love can I offer thee now
But love, darling, our love,
Yet tis as pure as thy pure brow
As pure as the Angels above.

(PAGE 183–188)
THE RAVEN
by Edgar A. Poe

Copied by Geo. Howard, Omaha Bks, Neb. from Ladies Reader of Prof. Howe's.

(PAGE 189–191)
Untitled poem by unknown author copied by Geo. S. Howard

(PAGE 192)
FAR FROM HOME
by J. V. McCoy
[J. V. McCoy wrote comments in George's diary that indicate she read it from cover to cover.]

(PAGE 193)
POWDER RIVER, Mar 17th 1876
Moccasin Joe

(PAGE 194)

"Did you see those Indians
*   Who lit out through the Ravine*
They did not act to me
*   As though they cared to be seen.*

"They must have a village
*   Over on Powder somewhere*
And they are looking around here
*   For any loose locks of hair."*

Thus the Scouts were talking
*   They had seen two Indians, you know*
Just what we had been hunting
*   For a couple of weeks or so.*

This meant hardship for us
*   More than you folks might think*
And for fifty hours we lived on
*   Just what we could get to drink.*

So we quickly to camp and made coffee
*   In our haste it was weak and stale*
Then up again and started out
*   Away on the Indian trail.*

You would scarce have thought the boys
*   All unused to trouble of course*
Would have made that cold night ride
*   Without a growl or a curse.*

But the boys were on their fight
*   Going for Redskins then and there*
Yet they must have known full well
*   That some of them would lose their hair.*

It was a hard night to ride
*   For thirty-five miles or so*
For all the time in our faces
*   Came a blinding, drifting snow.*

But that did not matter a bit
*   We had bothered with them too long*
And we vowed if we met any Indians
*   Their lives would not be worth a song.*

But after marching all night
*   And lying around in the cold*
We all began to think
*   That we had been badly sold.*

And we were nearly frozen
*   More especially our feet*
For the suffering of the seventeenth
*   Were mightly hard to beat.*

Till finally we heard they were found
*   And snug down on the River*
We started without a murmur
*   And hardly stopped to shiver*

At last we stopped again
*   And went through the Gulch on foot*
For we intended to kill those Redskins
*   And take all their stock to boot*

So we carefully crept away
*   To a good shooting distance*
And were ready to help the Greys
*   In case of great resistance.*

For sometime we stopped and watched Jimmy
    Get his Gray's down into the valley
Where they would be all ready
    At the sound of his cheering rally.

(PAGE 195)
Do you think in that forty-seven
    There was a heart for a moment quailed
No! they just thought of their Captain
    And they knew he never failed.

But I tell you it was hard
    To lie back there on the bluff
And see the Grays get ready
    To give it to the Indians rough

See how slowly they start the lines
    And gather up their Horses
They cannot all come back
    There re bound to be some losses

Trot! Gallop!! Charge!!!
    See how they start toward the Camp
For once the bloody devils
    Have got to get up and tramp

And now we break for the village
    To help wipe out the band
For they are as near Demons
    As any in the land.

For five hours we fought quite steady
    And never let up a bit
Yet don't know as we killed many Indians
    For you never could tell they were hit.

The well bear off the dead
    And take them out of our sight
And shooting so hot and heavy
    You cold not hear them screech.

(PAGE 196)
All this on the Seventeenth
    As no doubt you have heard before
And then we marched away
    Some eighteen miles or more.

And you bet the Reds feel bad
    For a hundred lodges were burned
And we took away seven hundred ponies
    As up the River we turned.

Now we are on the way back
    I trust to civilization
Our fight will be the talk
    The length and breadth of the nation.

But if they treat us fairly
    And give praise where it is due
Then it will be all right
    I think so, do not you?

(PAGE 197)
AN INCIDENT OF THE POWDER RIVER FIGHT

"Pard, they are getting too close
Well! I stopped one with that shot.
Let us go back to the boys
Where it isn't quite so hot."

By Jove, they have gone back somewhere
And I reckon we'd better git.
Do you suppose what made them skin
Was some of the boys getting hit?

Let's try for one more shot
We'll go up there top of the rise
I'm afraid I can't shoot straight
For that bullet rather blinded my eyes

By George, there lies Jack
He don't move—I'll bet he's shot
And the Reds are after his hair
But we'll give 'em hair of another sort.

There that last shot of mine
I know as done for one
Now let's get some help to carry Jack
Then I guess we'd better be gone.

I wish some of the boys were here
To help take him away

It beats hell they should leave him
With the Reds bad like today.

I say, Jack, where are you shot
Have the Indians fixed you this time?
By Jove, that's rather close
That bastard is shooting prime.

Well, old boy, it ain't very bad
But you see they don't always miss
Yet they are most damnable cowards
That would leave a man like this

Well, Pard, you take the guns
And I'll take the boy on my back
Just tell them I done my best
If they get me on my way back

Do you see that hole in my pants
That's pretty close sort of work
Yet they told me away down East
That I never was known to shriek.

Well, Pard, I guess they'll take care of him now
We've done the best we could
Now let's go back to the River
Right here in the edge of the wood.

Moccasin Joe of the Plains

(PAGE 199)
BEAUTIFUL HANDS
from Waverly Magazine

*Little by little I'm filling this book and I hope it
will serve to remind me in future years of my
troubles now.*

> Geo. S. Howard
> Co. "E" 2nd Cav.

(PAGE 200)
POWDER RIVER Mar. 17th 1876
G. S. Howard

*Twas on the day when every Son
Of Erins isle since time has run
Throws by dull care and every thought
Save those that are by ____ brought
Gives himself to pleasure up
And drowns the Shamrock in the Cup*

*That from the Otter's winding creek
And o'er Big Panthers Mountain steep
Rode Reynolds and as brave a band
As Ye'er drove spur or wielded brand
For do you know the Reds we'll seen
By Powder Rivers frozen stream*

*Full five and thirty miles we rode
Through cold that nearly froze the blood
For twenty-five degrees and more
Below as had been told before
But halted all at break of day
In cheerless pockets near our prey*

*Our Captains all were men of might
At lest if not in fighting quite
Had reputation in a way
That seemed quite fitting for the day
And carried neath their coats of blue
Of Pocket-Pistols not a few.*

*Like Grays that thought of Waterloo
"Wild Jimmy" formed his boys in blue*

*And on the Reds with ringing yell
His Troopers charged in gallant style
But Jimmy from in Border fray
Had oft been seen before that day
Twere well for Uncle Sam just then
His Army held some more such men*

(PAGE 201)
*Of one brave chief I fain would tell
Whose namesake at ____ fell
With pistol flourished high in air
He said while left hand grasped his hair
And o'er his brow there passed a gloom
"Come in Red son's of guns, Umph, Um."*

*Another Knight in Buckskin Blouse
Tried hard his lagging zeal to house
With nose six inches from the ground
And back to fight he ambled pound
And when safe distance he achieved
He shouted gladly, "I'm relieved."
When next the question we discuss
Relieve him just before the muss.*

*Five hours the battle raged and then
T'was thought we'd better move again
To safer quarters farther on
For don't you know discretion
The better part of valor is
He may fight again who runs from this*

*Tis not my mission to discourse
Of Cowardice or something worse
Displayed by shoulder straps that day
When we all knew they had the say
Enough! The soldier knew full well
Who blundered yet they dare not tell.*

Moccasin Joe

(PAGE 202)
WEARY

My life was clouded in darkness
Till your kindness illuminated the gloom
And I was sadly following the Pathway
That leads to the silent tomb
My life had been so unhappy
So beset by cares and fears
For joy had not been near me
For the numberless long years.

Your friendship has brightened the darkness
It has stilled my griefs and moans
And I now look forward with hope
For no more wild I be alone
My Spirits sweet vision of you
So young, beautiful and fair
Has drawn away all the sorrows
And banished to oblivion.
              Moccasin Joe (M.J.)

(PAGE 203)
DREAMING

Dreaming here in the sunlight
Of this glorious Autumn day
With no cares to oppress the mind
My thoughts oft go astray
They wander back to childhood
And happy days of yore
Those innocent youthful days
That ever come any more

That happy time in life's morning
Ere cares and troubles trace
Their wrinkles and their crows feet
Upon the fairest face

Childhood oft had its sorrows
Griefs that were hard to be borne
Yet though they troubled us greatly
They were all forgotten each morn.

Awakening from a night of slumber
That youthful slumber so sweet
We started anew on life's journey
On the race that is so fleet

We rush to the battle as swiftly
As did the Centaurs of old
And we are always racing for
That earthly treasure of gold

And forget in Life's bright morning
That treasure from above
That treasure so freely offered
The priceless boon of God's love

And oh! did we but realize
How more precious this might be
Would we not stop in our mad career
Our wild race to Eternity

Sometime of God we have plenty
But of God's treasure none
And we live but to regret
Yet this can never atone.

But if we in youthful days
Should gain God's treasure first
Then we fear neither grief or pain
Though they should do the worst

Moccasin Joe

(PAGE 204)
UNTITLED POEM
by Moccasin Joe

God help the wretch who nightly drags
Her life along the ghostly flags
In sin, in hunger, and in rags

God help her when the bitter rain
Beats on he as window pane
And nearly washes out her stain

God help her when with bleeding feet
She bows her head and stoops to meet
The cruel Wintry blast and sleet

God help her when with tearless eye
She looks into the darkened sky
And smiles her breast and asks to die

God help her wandering to and fro
Without one Christian smile to throw
A gleam upon her sullied brow

Poor child of ill, poor child of ill
A slave of her misguided will
God help her, she's a woman still.

God help her, George.
Moccasin Joe

(PAGE 205)
June 26th 1876

LINES WRITTEN ON THE DEATH OF GEN'L CUSTER AND MEN

Sadly we toll for the brave boys in blue
Who will ne'er again march in earthly review
Sadly we talk of their last gallant fight
Bodily battling for Country, for Freedom and Right
Of their brave deeds of valor, none ever shall tell
As slowly and sadly we toll their last knell

They have passed from our sight forever and aye
To that beautiful city of eternal day
In that last gallant charge who ever will tell
What thoughts filled each breast as each nobly fell
Perchance of Mother, Home, Children and Wife
And all they held dear in this Earthly life
For they passed from this earth midst carnage and death
The rifle reports and showers of lead
But each to the last was true to their flags
And ne'er for a moment allowed courage to lag
Their names will be sung with the braves of praise
And they'll ne'er be forgotten though they sleep in their graves

Moccasin Joe

[George Howard and his company learned of the Battle of the Little Big Horn while camping in the Black Hills along the Tongue River on July 10, the same day he mentions a battle with Indians in which he took part.]

(Page 206)
AT OLD FORT PHIL KEARNEY, June 6th, 1876

Here midst these storied ruins
How fast going to decay
My thoughts go back to those
Long since turned to kindred clay
I think of that brave party
Who fought so long and well
And who left not one of their number
Their deeds of valor to tell

In those days of bloody butchery
When life was held so cheap
Down in this pleasant valley
Here with their mountains steep.

When the Red Savage in his glory
Trampled upon land and right
Killed then all the children
Triumphing in his lowly might

And I think of that day of November
That caused many a heart to bleed
And a whole nation shuddered
When they heard of the horrible deed
Strong men went down in their manhood
Without a dying groan or word
and today brave hearts will grieve
When in the tale is heard

they rest near here together
But in that Home above
We trust they are rejoicing
In the mercy of God's Love

Moccasin Joe, The Poet of the Bad Lands
Moccasin Joe or Joe Reynolds, Louisville, Kentucky

[Fort Phil Kearny was established in July of 1866 and situated near present day Buffalo, Wyoming, in the heart of Indian hunting grounds in the north central portion of the state and along the Bozeman Trail. A great massacre took place December 21, 1866. The fort was abandoned in July of 1868 after much unrest from Indian tribes trying to regain their hunting grounds. George arrived at Fort Kearny at 7:30 a.m. on June 6, 1876, and noted a massacre of November 28, 1867.]

(PAGE 207)
MY PILLOW AND I

In the days and nights of disease and pain
It has cooled the fair of a wandering brain
It has turned one back when I seemed to stand
In the shadowy brink of another land—
Yes, tempted are back with its gentle caress
And soothed with its touches my cruel distress
Though others prove false, the world I defy
To part or estrange—My pillow and I

How brave and how strong in the world's
*   rough crowd*
Where men at the shrine of man are bowed
How glad and how gay in the glare of the day
When the din of trade drives sadness away!
And then how feeble and weary and lone
When nights black wing o'er the city is thrown
How cowardly weak as wakeful I lie
To know but to us my pillow and I.

Then the loves and the hates that I half forgot
In life's busy hours ere the sun has set
Are pondered o'er with a smile or a tear
And whispered names of the near and the dear

Or I humbly nurse on the wasted years
Of a vanished youth with its hopes and fears.
Till perchance I startle the night with a sigh
But we're used to that my pillow and I

We are right good friends, my pillow and I
I tell it my sorrows when no one is nigh
And it ne'er treats my confessions weak
But kisses in pity my feverish cheek
Nor ever recoiled with a feigned alarm
From the rough embrace of my weary arm
But gives me repose no treasure can buy
A sacred tie binds us, my pillow and I

I know full well in the watches we key
Trail—a whispered prayer and reluctant sleep
It knows full well how the shadows last
Which passion and pride o'er the hearty
home cast
And it blots the tears that are vainly shed
Air hopes destroyed and ambitions dead
Then it brings forgetfulness by and by
And we dream in peace, my pillow and I.

[The poem about George's pillow is especially touching when readers know that he slept on his diary during his enlistment. The first verse was written on page 206 before the title and remaining verses were penned on page 207.]

(PAGE 208)
TEMPTATION
by Unknown author

(PAGE 209)
THE BEAUTIFUL PAST

Methinks it were sweet on this golden day
To close my eyes and soar way,
*   To the beautiful past once more.*
To forget that the world is proud and cold,
'Mid care and strife, I'm growing old
*   And the beautiful past is o'er.*

Methinks it were sweet on the troubled way
To hold to my heart each glimmering ray
*   Of my childhood summer time:*
To forget that youth has faded away:
And as twilight dispense to wearing gray
*   So fades our youth summer time.*

Yet methinks it is sweet in the evening gray
To catch but a gleam of returning day:
*   Ere life in this world is o'er:*
To forgive and forget, to love, not regret.
*   To live o'er the past once more.*

(PAGE 210)
IN MY HEART

Go join in the glittering crowd
*   And laugh with the merriest there*
Go bind the brows of thy Summer friends
*   With garlands and roses fair*
But come when the roses fade
*   And each thorn has left its smart*
For I have a sprig of forget-me-nots
*   I am wearing for thee in my heart.*

Aye go where thy spirits are light
*   Seeking others as wild and free*
And find if thou canst another one
*   That always thine own will be*
But come if thy search is vain
*   And thy weariness paineth for rest*

I'll keep thee a home in my changeless love
*   And pillow thy head on my breast.*

Moccasin Joe

LEAF BY LEAF THE ROSES FALL
Moccasin Joe

Leaf by leaf the roses fall
*   Drop by drop the springs run dry*
One by one beyond recall
*   Summer beauties fade and dry*
But the roses bloom again
*   And the springs will gush anew*
In the pleasant April rain
*   And the Summers Sun.*

So in hours of deepest gloom
*   Where the Springs of gladness fail*
and the roses in their bloom
*   Droop like maidens wane and pale,*
We shall find some hope that lies
*   Like some silent germ apart*
Hidden far from careless eyes
*   In the Garden of the heart.*

(PAGE 211)
Some sweet hope to gladness wed
*   That will spring afresh and new*
When Winter shall have fled
*   Giving place to sun and dew*
Some sweet hope that breathes of Spring
*   Through the weary, weary time*
Budding forth its blossoming
*   In the spirit's gentle cling.*

(PAGE 212)
THE BACHELOR'S SOLILOQUY

Marry or not to marry. That is the question.
Whether tis nobler in the mind to suffer
The sullen silence of these cobweb rooms
Or seek in festive halls some cheerful dame
And by uniting end it. To live alone
No more. And by marrying say we end
The heartaches and those throes and makeshifts
Bachelors are heir to. Tis a consummation
Devoutly to be wished.
To marry—to live in peace—
Perchance in war—ay, there's the rub!
For in the marriage state what ills may come
When we have shuffled off our liberty
Must give us pause. There's the respect
That makes as dread the bond of wedding.
For who could bear the noise of scolding wives
The fits of spleen. The extravagance of dress
The thirst for plays, for concerts, and for balls
The insolence of servants and the spurns
That patient husbands from their consorts take
When he himself might his quietus gain
By living single?
Who would wish to bear
The jarring name of bachelor
But the dread of something after marriage
Oh, the vast expenditure of income
Tongue can scarcely tell, puzzles the will
And makes us rather choose the single life
than go to jail for debts we know not of!
Economy thus makes bachelors of us still
And thus our melancholy resolution
Is still increased upon more various thought

Moccasin Joe
Howard
Co "E" 2nd Cavalry
Fort Sanders,
Wyoming

ONE AT HOME WHO PRAYS FOR ME
Geo. (George Howard)

At midnight on my lonely beat
The shadows wrap the wood and lo
A vision comes my view to great
Of one at home who prays for me
No roses bloom upon her brow
Her form is not a lover's dream
But in that brow so pure and meek
A thousand holier beauties gleam.

How softly shines her silver hair
A patient smile is on her face
and that mild, lustrous light of prayer
Around her sheds a moonlight grace
She prays for me so far away
A soldier in his holy fight
And begs that heaven in mercy may
Protest her boy and bless the right.

Still thought the leagues lie far between
This silent incense of her heart
Steals o'er my sole with brow serene
And we no longer are apart
So guarding this my lonely beat
By shadowy wood and haunted den
That vision comes my view too great
Of her at home who prays for me

(Page 213 to 216, two pages, are missing from original diary.

(PAGE 217)
Fort Sanders Jan 1877

There are some of the people around here who think I am nothing but a plaything for them to make fun of. Let them look out for themselves, the Crazy Captain of Warriors is one of the things they must beware of and there are many in the haunts of the Comanche Tribe who can tell them the same.   Joe Reynolds

Known as

George S. Howard   (This signature cut from diary)
Serg 1 Co "E" 2nd Cav'y
Fort Sanders
Wyoming

Fort Sanders Wyo Feb 14th 1877
Another marriage project bust up and I have only 8 months from today!

Joe Reynolds

Feb. 26th   Make my last visit to Lizzie tonight. Well, it's best to be off with the old love before you are on with the new.

Joe Reynolds

[The Lizzie he mentions in this entry refers to Elizabeth "Lizzie" Stevens of Laramie City who he dated while stationed at Fort Sanders. He mentions her in various places throughout the diary, and says that he and Lizzie were married. This marriage never took place.]

78

(PAGE 218)

[George created a very detailed index of the poems in his diary and that index is reproduced below.]

Index to Scout's Book of Howard

(PAGE 219)

(Index Continued)

* Poems written by Geo. Howard or Moccasin Joe *[This footnote was written by George Howard but the "*" do not reflect the actual number of poems he wrote.]*

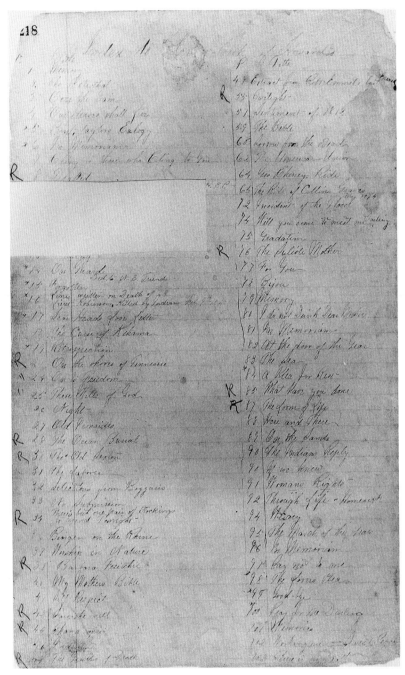

Page 218 of George S. Howard's diary is the start of his poetry index. The missing piece in the upper left corner was removed by his wife when she applied for a widow's pension in 1931.

Page 219 of the original diary is a continuation of the poetry index on page 218.

Chapter Five

Treasured Scraps at the Back of the Diary

Scraps of newspaper clippings from the early 1900s were found tucked inside the 257-page diary between the final page and back cover.

The first clipping shows a photograph of Chief Washakie (Shoots-the Buffalo-Running) whom George Howard knew as the main Indian guide during the 1876 summer campaign. The clipping shows the Shoshone camp along the Wind River Mountains, Wyoming, where George hunted for elk and deer in 1872 and 1873.

The clipping notes that 1,000 Shoshones remained on the reservation at Wind River but no date on the newspaper clipping is visible. According to the article, Chief Washakie was born of an Arapahoe mother about 1804 and died in early 1900. He was buried with military honors at Fort Washakie on the Shoshone-Arapahoe Reservation in Wyoming. He was known as a terror to the Blackfeet and Crow Indians and a friend to the white men.

A second clipping shows an illustration of Fort Laramie in 1836, which had been collected by the Wyoming Historical Society. The sketch was based upon a sketch drawn during the Fremont Expedition in the 1840s. The newspaper clipping says, "One hundred years ago in 1834," indicating the paper was from 1934. Most likely, Grace Howard Porter or her mother Martha collected the clippings.

The caption reads: "One hundred years ago, in 1834, the Oregon Trail was existent, but nameless; Fort Laramie, in process of construction by the fur traders, was called Fort William. Built of adobe, at the junction of the Laramie and the North Platte, it was destined to become a famous point on the great trail of covered wagon days."

A third clipping is dated November 29, 1964, and has Grace Howard Porter's handwriting across the headline. The newspaper is not identified. The article regards the last sixteen Indian War soldiers. According to this article, as of 1964, the Veterans Administration reported that of the 106,000 men who fought during the 40-year Indian wars in the West, sixteen men remained. The youngest was 83 and the oldest was 103. Battles with Indians began in an organized fashion in 1865 when the Army turned its attention to the West after the Civil War. The last major battle was in 1898. The most active portion of the Indian Wars took place in 1876, the article said.

A final clipping provided insight into the cost of the Indian Wars. The clipping, from the *Boston Journal* on June 29, 1880, reported that $180,000 had been spent in the last decade of the Indian War. The editorial reads, "Perhaps, if the white man had always been just in his dealings with the Indian, all those wars with their terrible cost in money, misery, and bloodshed

Headquarters Fort Sanders, Wyoming.

May 2?
187?

The Last Farewell.

I am dying, Annie, dying,
   And my life is going fast;
Hushed forever is my sighing,
   Death has claimed his own at last.

Life for me had lost its pleasure,
   I was tired living on;
Tho' I've trod not half its measure,
   I have trod it all alone.

When I knew you life was brighter
   Than before for many a year;
But broken soon will be the fetter,
   That has bound me so long here

And my last wish as I lie here,
   Slowly going to my death,
Is that you may shed a tear,
   When you hear of this my death.

The first page of George's poem, "The Last Farewell," was sent to his mother in Hinsdale, New Hampshire, on May 29, 1877, two days before he left Fort Sanders for home. The poem was dedicated to his girlfriend Johanna Delinde.

might have been avoided. For there is good reason to believe that in nearly every instance some act or series of acts of injustice or wrong done by whites, officials, or the reckless settlers of the border against the Indians have caused the opening of hostilities. It is an open question, and although retrospective, may be made profitable if its discussion shall help to the adoption of more humane, less expensive, and more efficacious Indian policy on the part of our Government and our people."

Several letters written by George and saved by his mother were placed inside the diary along with the news clippings. Their exact translations are reprinted below.

THE LAST FAREWELL

[The letter is dated May 29, 1877, Fort Sanders, Wyoming, on the fort's letterhead stationery. George was honorably discharged from the Army on May 31, 1877, and returned by train to Hinsdale, New Hampshire.]

I am dying, Annie, dying
And my life is going fast;
Hushed forever is my sighing,
Death has claimed his own at last.

Life for one had lost its pleasure,
I was tired living on;
Tho' I've lived not half its measure,
I have trod it all alone.

When I knew you life was brightest
Than before for many a year;
But broken soon will be the letter,
That has bound me so long here.

And my last wish as I lie here
Slowly going is my breath
Is that you may shed a tear,
When you hear of this my death.

That you may remember kindly,
The old time of long ago;
For I loved you, oh! so blindly,
In the midst of my deep woe.

But farewell, breath is going;
Life's dark journey's nearly o'er;
I am slowly, surely sinking, knowing,
That Death's knocking on the door.
Moccasin Joe
Dedicated to Johanna DeLinde

Fort Laramie?
March 10th 1873

Dear Mother

It is just as pleasant
day as you ever saw. I am almost in my shirt
sleeves for the thermometer is up to 80 upon
etc and the sun shines just as bright as it
ever did on a spring day in New England
More poetry

Bright thoughts on the plains

To a lone starry night on the Prairie
With the coyotes howling wild
And the calm blue sky is covering
I'm a bold New England child
There's trouble on the border now
And we have left the fort
To punish the thieving Savage
Though blood may be the cost
... in this Border Warfare
Full many a form is left

There is some more to come but
I have not room for it in this letter
I did not get my [?] in this pay
day but think I shall next
But the mail came my today
and I will write some
I want to know where Lucina is,
and Antunms address will to
Ellen whose I am and have her
and Effie write to me I wish Effie
would pay you that $10 The Indians
are going to act bad this spring I
guess. I do not suppose you know
any thing about it from the papers
you get I wish you would send my
[?] I shall keep some names
a while that's in this all the
mail that came was a letter
from Ellen and I can't remember
tis to night foot write her, I will
some time. I am going to Laramie
Peak to in when 1/5 in this so

George S. Howard wrote this letter to his mother four months after he arrived at Fort Laramie, Wyoming Territory. Two of the four pages are shown here.

NIGHT THOUGHTS ON THE PLAINS

[This letter and poem was written to his mother at Fort Laramie on March 10, 1873, four months after George arrived in Wyoming to begin his five-year enlistment.]

Dear Mother,

It is just as pleasant a day as you ever saw. I am around in my shirt sleeves for the thermometer is up in temperature and the sun shines just as bright as it ever did on a spring day in New England.

More poetry.

Tis a lone starry night on the Prairie
With the coyotes howling wild
And the calm blue sky is covering
For a bold New England child
There is trouble on the border now
And we have left the post
And blood may be the cost
For in this Border Warfare
Full many a form is left.

There is some more to come but I have not room for it in this letter. I did not get my debt in this payday but think I shall next. But the mail came in today and I will write some.

I want to know where Lucius is, and Auburn's address. Write to Ellen where I am and have her and Effie write to me. I wish Effie would pay you that $10. The Indians are going to act bad this spring, I guess. I do not suppose you know anything about it from the papers you get. I wish you would send me names a while. That is all the mail that came in was a letter from Ellen and I cannot answer it in tonight's post. Write her. I will sometime. I am going to Laramie Peak. I have not got that box of stationary and do not send it. Wait a reasonable time to hear from me before you send anything. Also, I have got $11 owing to me here and if I ever get that I never shall lend anymore. I will send it home.

Best wishes to all the Girls. Good bye.

Geo. Howard
Company E, 2nd Cav.
Fort Laramie, Wyo.

[His sisters included Amy (4/14/1830–10/30/1898), Melissa (2/19/1832–1/16/1907), Philena (1/20/1834–11/21/1888), Hannah May (11/25/1839–1894), Celinda Jane (12/24/1843–5/9/1848), Ellen Maria (3/4/1847–12/28/1916), and Anne Auburn (7/13/1852–2/9/1919).

Brothers to George included Cyrus (9/27/1828–1/12/1870), Seymour (4/4/1836–6/25/1916), Lucius (2/17/1838-born and died), Henry Milton (3/25/1842–11/27/1913), James (6/10/1845–6/24/1863), and Walter Royal (6/20/1854–8/29/1854). Since Walter and Lucius died as infants, George was the youngest of the seven sons who lived to adulthood.]

Chapter Six

What To Do with a 120-Year-Old Diary?

I will never forget that cold January day in 1977 when I received a brown box from the United Parcel Service delivery man. He knocked on my front door in Arlington, Virginia, and asked me to sign for the unassuming cardboard package.

My uncle in Chicago, Jack Strohm, had said he was sending me something very old and very special, so when the package arrived, I immediately opened it. There, beneath a layer of protective newspapers was a fragile ledger book, measuring 9- by 13-inches and containing 257 yellowed pages and fragments of newspaper clippings and letters. Nothing separated the crumbling pages from the cold January air.

The UPS man stood speechless when I told him this was the daily diary of a cavalry scout named George Shepard Howard who lived in the West from 1872 to 1877. The UPS man left hurriedly to deliver a truckload of other packages, but seemed impressed that he had handled such a priceless document.

I was pregnant with my first child, a son, who was born on March 22, 1977. A few days after receiving the diary, I waddled to the National Archives in early February to begin my 14-year investigation of the diary and its author. During the time period I conducted the research and preservation of this wonderful diary, I delivered three sons who have all helped me in the investigations over the years as they grew and matured. I also authored and edited two other books between 1983 and 1993 and wrote thousands of articles for newspapers and magazines.

Researching the diary became my ongoing quest to uncover the pulse and spirit of George S. Howard who signed all his diary entries as Moccasin Joe, hence the title of this book. I wanted young people to appreciate American history through the pages of this diary, so I included my sons in the project whenever I could. Here was a young man bursting with an adventurous spirit who fell in love, was injured, faced deadly battles, hunted and fished throughout Wyoming, the Dakotas, and Montana, and coped with Frontier life and a pounding headache. I wanted my young sons to recognize that a young man from the 19th century had the same emotions and feelings they had. They had a connection with another century, and I wanted other young people to feel that connection, too.

My Uncle Jack is a great letter writer and had grown to know the diary writer's daughter, Grace Howard Porter. Through active correspondence, Grace had mentioned her father's diary. Jack introduced me to Grace in 1976 when she was 96, and the three of us continued a lively correspondence until her death at age 98 on July 19, 1979.

Uncle Jack is an avid reader and had researched the Indian tribes of the West, but had limited access to the Old Army records related to George. He had transcribed small portions of the prose section of the diary with the help of his daughter, and my first cousin, Alice. He was happy to know I wanted to devote more time to the research.

Grace knew her time on earth was ending, so in a letter she asked Jack and me if we would ever want her father's diary. She had no children or grandchildren, and Jack and I were cousins. Her father was my great, great, great uncle. She knew from our letters to her that we were lovers of American history.

She told us she wanted the diary to go to someone who would appreciate its pages. From the bottom of a storage trunk in her house, Grace wrapped the diary in brown paper and mailed it in late 1976 to Uncle Jack—no insurance or tracking numbers. Shortly after receiving this massive document, Jack asked me to take the diary and do the necessary research since I had easy access to the documents and historians from the National Archives, Smithsonian Institution, and Library of Congress.

At the time, although I was seven months pregnant, I worked as a tour guide for the Smithsonian Institution and had trained with the curators of American history. Throughout 1977 and long after John Reneau was born, I sat in front of microfiche machines on the second floor of the National Archives and read U.S. Army documents or reviewed photographs on the 18th floor of the National Archives building in the still picture section.

Grace continued to share the details of her father's life, and I found her recollections distinct and moving. She was especially delighted to discover two relatives of hers appreciated her father's diary and wanted to do something with it. One of the letters I treasure most is when she told me that she was thrilled to hear I planned to write a book based upon the diary.

Preserving the Fragile Diary

My first task after receiving the treasured diary was to permanently preserve the disintegrating pages. The pages at the beginning and end of the document were badly frayed, and the blue ink was fading to pale lavender throughout the diary. The binding of the ledger book had fallen apart and threads were hanging from the cover. Thanks to the patient teachings of Robert E. McComb of the preservation, research, and testing office of the Library of Congress, I was shown how to encapsulate each page of the diary and the front and back covers with a non-acidic plastic covering called mylar. A non-acidic, double-stick tape manufactured by the 3M Company was used to press the mylar together. I purchased the plastic and tape from the Hollinger Corp. of Arlington, Virginia, and went about the business of preservation.

Each page of the diary was sandwiched between two oversized pieces of the clear, mylar plastic, held together by double-stick, non-acidic tape. No portion of each page touched the tape. Each of the pages was sealed inside the mylar. This simple process kept air, dust, hand oils, and other damaging particles away from the paper without destroying the document. I spent two weeks encapsulating the diary and other papers and letters found inside it. The entire diary remains encapsulated in this same protective covering today—perfectly preserved.

Fort Sanders Jan 1877
There are some of the people around
here who think I am nothing but a plaything
for them to make fun off let them look out for
themselves the Crazy Captive of "Wm Bails" is one
of the things they must be ware of, and there
are many in the haunts of the Camanche
tribe who can tell them the same   Jos Reynolds
Known as

Jos Reynolds

Fort Sanders Wyo Feb. 18th
Another Marriage project busted up and
I have only 8 class from to day
Jos Reynolds
Feb 26th Make my last visit to Lizzie
tonight Well to best to be off with the old love
ere you are on with the new
Jos Reynolds

Page 217 of the diary was written at Fort Sanders in 1877. The missing piece was located in the widow's pension file at the National Archives in 1979.

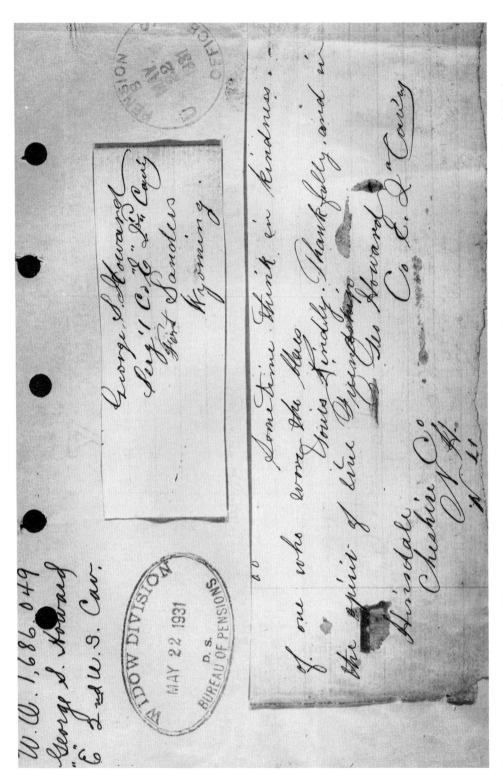

The missing piece from Page 217 of George's diary includes his full signature, military rank, and where he was stationed. The lower scrap of paper is from a letter home to his mother. It reads, "Sometime think in kindness of one who has wore the blues. Yours Kindly, Thankfully and in the spirit of true Friendship, Geo. Howard, Co. E. 2nd Cav'ry, Hinsdale, Cheshire Co., N.H."

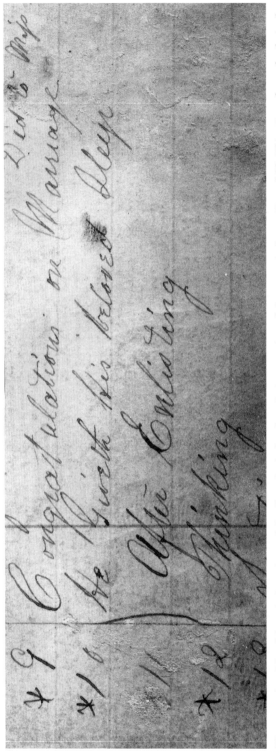

The opposite side of the missing piece of the diary includes the missing portion of the poem index on Page 218. This piece fit perfectly in the hole left after his widow removed it in 1931.

157

Uncovering the Mystery of Diary Messages

Next, I needed to locate someone to help me research the contents of the diary from a historical perspective. I didn't find *someone*. I found many *someones*.

My exploration of history from 1977 to 1991 brought me in direct contact with some of the greatest minds of America on the subjects of Western and military history. I spoke to Herman Viola and Kathleen Baxter of the National Anthropological Archives of the Smithsonian Institution to review Indian photographs and pictographs and to study reference books. I interviewed James Hanson of the Native American Program of the Smithsonian Institution.

I received valuable assistance from Terry Gray, a Sioux Indian and administrator from Sinte Galska College, Rosebud, South Dakota, who was an intern at the Smithsonian in 1990 and who identified Indian outfits, language expressions, and subtle symbolisms of the Indian cultures depicted in rare tintype and stereoscopic photographs. His ancestors were in the Sioux tribes my diary writer knew in the early 1870s, which made my conversations with Terry all the more special. His ancestors could have easily spoken to Moccasin Joe over the course of his five-year enlistment. Terry called a friend of his, the great grandson of Spotted Tail, about the availability of Indian illustrations of Indian War battles, but discovered none existed.

Reading material for my studies began with the information given to me in 1977 by Charles E. Hanson, Jr., who is director of the Museum of the Fur Trade in Chadron, Nebraska. His list of books became the foundation for my research as I learned the ins and outs of Frontier life of Indians and white men.

At the National Archives, over a period of fourteen years, I was enthusiastically assisted by many men and women who work there. I have found volumes of personnel papers, enlistment documents, rare military maps, and photographs. Archivists from the military reference branch located microfilmed records of regiment activities and original military reports and letters. Old Army archivists Mike Musick, Mike Meir, and William E. Lind persistently led me to rare documents that unearthed volumes of personal history on George S. Howard and his commanding officers, including Gen. George Crook, Gen. William T. Sherman, Col. Joseph J. Reynolds, Capt. Elijah R. Wells, Capt. Anson Mills, Lt. Frederick W. Sibley, Capt. Henry E. Noyes, Capt. Alexander Moore, and Capt. James Egan. Starting in the winter of 1977, I met with Mike, Mike and Bill to investigate letters, personnel files, maps, photographs, and military reports that pieced together the meaning of George's poetry and prose.

Others at the National Archives who have assisted me in my search over the years were Constance Potter, Dee Cartright, Gene Dear, Tod J. Butler, Trudy Peterson, and Lee Bacon. Mario Lopez Feliu, book binder in the document reproduction and preservation department of the National Archives in 1977, first tested the diary pages and discovered that the rag paper contained traces of horse and human blood. Mr. Feliu showed me the process of encapsulation and directed me to preservationists at the Library of Congress and the National Archives who taught me the proper techniques.

Mr. Feliu's chemical analysis of the pages provided insight into the activities of George S. Howard based upon the dirt, ink, and blood on the pages of his journal. He introduced me to Graeme A. McCluggage in the encapsulation department of the National Archives who taught me the basics of preservation in 1977.

One of the most memorable events of my life occurred in February of 1979 when I found George S. Howard's original enlistment papers and his widow's pension file. For years, I had wondered why a small 1- by 2-inch piece of a page was missing from pages 217 and 218 of the diary. When I opened the pension file, a small, 1- by 2-inch piece of yellowed paper fell to the reading room table containing George S. Howard's signature on one side and index listings on the other. The next evening, I asked the reading room supervisor at the National Archives if I could bring my diary page to the room and verify that the small piece belonged in the diary. Sure enough, when I placed the small piece of paper beside the diary page, the piece fit perfectly. This missing diary piece, safely stored with George's military records since the early 1900s, proves without a doubt that he wrote the diary. The Archives staff photographed the missing piece as an illustration for this book. The Archives staff in the reading room were speechless when they saw how the tiny missing piece fit back into the diary after being separated for almost a century.

George's widow, Martha Colburn Howard, cut the piece from the diary to prove his signature matched the wedding certificate and enlistment papers she submitted to the U.S. Army to receive a pension of $30 per month. In the pension file, Martha had also submitted family genealogical records, death and marriage certificates, and letters from family and friends to prove she had been married to a cavalry soldier who served in Montana, Wyoming, the Dakotas and Nebraska from 1872 to 1877. The discovery of the widow's pension file was one of the most valuable in my quest for information about the diary. Finding this file would not have been possible without the help of the Archive's staff. If his wife, Martha, had not been so diligent in her quest for the pension, all of the information about George S. Howard's life would have remained a mystery. Unfortunately for Martha, she died in 1935 and collected only a small amount of the pension due her.

Significant to my quest for information about Moccasin Joe's life were the chatty letters written to my uncle and to me by Grace beginning in 1975. Before Grace died, she described to me the details of her father's Western adventures, married life with Martha, a secret Civil War enlistment as a drummer boy, a serious railroad accident that crushed his head, and his premature death by murder at age 36.

Grace delighted in letter writing. She was a breed of ladies from the Victorian era who relished in the detailed descriptions of her experiences and the experiences of the people she knew and loved. Without her letters I never would have been able to piece together the parts of Moccasin Joe's life. She told of a train accident before his Army enlistment and of his attempts to run away from home at age 11 to join the Army using the age of his older brother James, who also joined the Army during the Civil War and died in 1863.

Brief comments by Grace led me to uncover newspaper accounts of the train accident of 1870 and his murder in 1887 by reviewing newspaper issues on microfilm at the Library of Congress. Her descriptions of his railroad experiences led me to the Association of American Railroads (AAR), where I found original 19th-century books that clarified his life experiences. The AAR library contained books with descriptions of medical procedures and railroad accidents from the 1800s plus train schedules and tourist guides describing Western landmarks and cities George visited and lived in during his Western adventures. Grace's letters allowed me to create a clear biographical sketch of her father. She was only six when her father was shot in the neck, so much of what she revealed were stories she heard from her older sister and mother. Her strongest memory was the day her father died, and she relived the experience through her letters to me.

Fourteen years were spent by my husband, Jack Reneau, and me in the National Archive's microfilm reading room studying regimental rolls and activity reports, locating the personnel records of commanding officers, and studying the rare military maps and photographs. To locate George's Civil War file, I had to cross reference hundreds of feet of microfilm that listed Union soldiers from New Hampshire, Vermont, Maine, Rhode Island, and Massachusetts where he might have joined since the distance between his New Hampshire home and other New England states was so small.

Some of the most difficult moments came when George made a vague reference to an event in history that was occurring for him at that very moment but that had no meaning for me. Reading dozens of Western history books provided me with clues to George's comments. Some of the more helpful books are listed in the annotated bibliography of this book. I recommend them all.

Over the years, my husband, Jack, joined me in the quest for information. Jack read hundreds of newspaper entries and scanned the card files of the Library of Congress until he found the newspaper accounts of George's train accident and death. We wrote to the Fitchburg Library in Fitchburg, Massachusetts, and requested information about George's life in that railroad town where he worked for the Vermont and Massachusetts Railroad and the Fitchburg Railroad. When Jack wasn't reviewing books and microfilm, he was babysitting three active toddlers as I scanned the Library of Congress and National Archives stacks of paperwork. We took turns watching our sons as the research files piled higher and higher.

Jack spent many weekends and evenings reviewing articles and military records in the National Archives and Library of Congress that helped piece together parts of George S. Howard's short life. Jack patiently scanned library files until he was satisfied he had the correct articles; then he copied the rare articles for our research files. Some of the original newspapers are only accessible on microfilm, the remaining original copies being too fragile to handle. We were grateful for the technology of microfilm.

A visit to Hinsdale, New Hampshire, and Athol, Massachusetts, in 1991 netted for us the last will and testament of Cyrus Howard, father to George, family documents, and a photograph of the train wreck that crushed George's head. The photograph, found in the Athol Historical Society Museum by Curator Dexter Gleason, is reproduced in this book and shows the extent of damage to the train's engine and passenger cars. On that visit to Hinsdale, Jack stood on a hillside overlooking the tiny town and met the family who lives in George Howard's home— the home Cyrus Howard built in the early 1850s after his marriage to Louisa. Jack visited the grave sites of the Howard family, including George's; and worked with Athol photographer Bob Mayer to reproduce the original train accident tintype.

Some of the people who helped us find our reading list were Col. William G. Bell, historian for the U.S. Army; Professor Henry Taylor, historian at American University, Washington, D.C.; Professor Peter Hill, historian at George Washington University, Washington, D.C.; Pamela E. Zimmerman, librarian at the Association of American Railroads, Washington, D.C.; Al Minnick, former librarian and archivist for the Buffalo Bill Historical Center, Cody, Wyoming; James S. Hutchins, armed forces historian at the National Museum of American History, Smithsonian Institution, Washington, D.C.; and John J. Slonaker, chief of the historical reference section of the U.S. Army Military History Institute, Carlisle Barracks, Pennsylvania.

Also helpful in locating newspaper accounts, death certificates, and autopsy reports was Eleanora West, curator of the Fitchburg Historical Library, Fitchburg, Massachusetts. She and her staff reproduced original articles from the *Fitchburg Sentinel* that further clarified the life and death of George S. Howard.

Finding illustrations for the diary presented a special challenge. I found a large cache of rare maps and photographs at the Library of Congress, Smithsonian Institution, and National Archives, but felt there were other illustrations in the West. My research led me to the Denver Public Library Western History Department. The entire series of photographs taken by famed Western photographer, Stanley J. Morrow, during the Big Horn Expedition, were discovered and some of those stereoscopic views illustrate this book. Helping me find the photographs were A. D. Mastrogiuseppe, Lisa Backman, Kay Wisnia, and Nancy Case.

I quickly discovered that only a few photographs of this time period exist, and that the National Archives had many of the same Morrow photographs that are in the Denver Public Library collection, so photo credits sometimes became a little tricky.

Staff from the Buffalo Bill Historical Center in Cody, Wyoming, provided identification of rare photographs and comments in the diary in 1990. They also helped me trace George's footsteps in the Carter Mountains near Cody and the Bighorn River Basin where he hunted and fished. They also helped me locate the approximate location of where George and a friend, referred to as "Pard" in the diary, encountered grizzly bear in south Yellowstone National Park in the winter of 1872 and 1873.

Staff at the Buffalo Bill Historical Center who helped me identify references and photographs were Joan Murra and Elizabeth A. Brink. Elizabeth had just completed an article about the clothing of Mary Canary Burke, known as Calamity Jane, who rode as a man with Gen. George Crook as a teamster and guide during the Big Horn Expedition. Joan located references on Buffalo Chips who was a friend of Buffalo Bill killed at the Battle of Slim Buttes. George S. Howard mentions the death of Buffalo Chips in his diary and the discovery of Calamity Jane as a teamster. George S. Howard was one of the soldiers who rode with these Western characters during the Big Horn Expedition.

As my 14-year research project came to a close in August of 1991, I felt remorse that the quest was over. Now it was my responsibility to put this research to work as a tale of lost love, found courage, and lost life for one man who called himself Moccasin Joe.

Chapter Seven

Walking in the Footsteps of Moccasin Joe

To complete my understanding of Moccasin Joe, I wanted to walk in his footsteps and experience the scenery he experienced as he wrote poems and prose. It was important for us to visit Fort Laramie, Fort Fetterman, Big Horn Mountains, Little Big Horn River, Lake DeSmet, and the Yellowstone National Park where Moccasin Joe spent so much of his time from 1872 to 1877. On my adventure to Wyoming in the summer of 1990, I brought along my 13-year-old son, John, who was with me when I first received the diary in 1977. Our family moved to Missoula, Montana, in September of 1992, so we took our three sons, John (age 15), Robert (age 12), and Richard (age 10), to the Little Big Horn Battlefield National Monument and crossed geographic landmarks and forts Moccasin Joe described in his diary including Deadwood, Goose Creek, Crazy Woman River, Powder River, Fort Reno, and Fort Phil Kearny. I wanted my sons to experience the wildness and remoteness Moccasin Joe had experienced 120 years earlier in hopes that other young people would read the pages of this rare diary, and marvel at another young person's adventure and agony from another century.

As we drove down lonely roads in our metal and plastic Toyota station wagon in 1990, John would read portions of the diary while we crossed landmarks George mentioned. In one week in August of 1990, John and I covered most of the distance George covered in five years on horseback. George arrived eighteen years before Wyoming became a state in 1890, so it seemed appropriate that I brought my son back to Wyoming in its centennial year.

We noted how similar the landscapes and forts of Laramie and Fetterman remained compared to his diary descriptions, and marveled that the scenic beauty of Wyoming and Montana remained similar to his descriptions from 1872. John found George's descriptions of rivers and rock formations especially accurate compared to what he was seeing in 1990. Some of George's descriptions were so close to what we were experiencing that I felt chills up and down my spine. John felt the same thing.

Headed towards Fort Laramie from Cheyenne, riding our 60-horsepower station wagon, John and I reached the post in two hours, after covering 105 miles along the modern highways of Interstate 25 and Route 26. George spent four days on horseback traveling the same distance after first arriving in Cheyenne by the Union Pacific Railroad in October of 1872 as a new recruit. Horse miles traveled were 95 for George.

Majestically rising 10,272 feet above sea level, Laramie Peak still dominates the landscape as we approached the exit to Fort Laramie. This single, dominating peak is a part of the

John Reneau climbs rocks near the Shoshone River outside Cody, Wyoming, in 1990 in the same area where George S. Howard hiked, hunted, and fished in 1872 and 1873. John retraced Moccasin Joe's footsteps using the diary entries as a guide.

Laramie Peak still dominates the plains near Fort Laramie as it did when George S. Howard lead wagon trains on the Oregon Trail.

Laramie Mountains George explored for five years and recommended heartily as a place to hunt for various wild game. Antelope looked up from grazing as we passed, showing their white rumps as a signal to run. Outcroppings of barren rock, rolling hills, and royal blue skies laced with horsetail clouds graced our vision for as far as we could see.

Few houses blocked our view. Sandstone hillsides, carved by prairie winds, added slight variations to the quiet beauty of Wyoming. These same scenes fill the descriptions in George's journal. We reached Fort Laramie in the afternoon of our first day and discovered that many of the same buildings George had used throughout his enlistment were fully restored by the National Park Service. We were able to walk inside the cavalry barracks he helped to construct in 1874 and visit with a modern woman who played the part of the fort laundress.

John and I sat and listened to a banjo and fiddle player entertain visitors on the wide veranda of "Old Bedlam," the bachelor officers' quarters, just as George would have enjoyed in 1872. We listened to "The Girl I Left Behind," "Soldier's Joy," "Marching through Georgia," and "Sweet Betsy from Pike," favorite tunes of the Western recruit. These were the same songs George would have heard and sung around a campfire or beside his cavalry barracks. Many of the songs from the Civil War continued as favorites for the Western recruits.

As the sun set in the distance, John and I imagined George smiling to himself as he caught monster trout in the river and sang songs of lost love and past battles near "Old Bedlam." A slight breeze messed our hair as we entered the fort bakery, the 1876 guardhouse, and the 1875 post surgeon's quarters. We entered the post's store that provided extra supplies to troops throughout the fort's existence. The north side of the store, built of stone in 1852, served as a post office for the troops and settlers, so it would have been here that George received and sent letters from home. John and I sat in the stone building sipping a soda pop and imagining George's reaction to all these modern visitors. John especially enjoyed visiting the bakery where loaves of bread were coming out of the oven. He imagined George eagerly waiting at the mess hall for his dinner and savoring the aroma of the bread.

Based upon a rare map of Fort Laramie found in the National Archives dating from 1874, George probably lived in the barracks across the Laramie River from "Old Bedlam," barracks that do not exist today. The map shows cavalry barracks across from the parade ground beside the tents of the unit laundress. We were unable to cross the river to the place where George lived, but we stood silently and visualized the barracks that faced the river.

George lived at the fort full-time from 1872 to 1874 and traveled through the fort from 1875 to 1877 on various campaigns. He mentions watching a river flow past his barrack window. We stood beside the gentle Laramie River and watched as water splashed over weathered rocks protecting small fish. Was this the same spot where George fished and wrote his poetry? Maybe so, John thought.

John and I enjoyed the conversation and knowledge of Steven R. Fullmer, fort manager, who provided valuable insight into the workings of the restored fort. We visited the library where George stood more than a hundred years ago to copy favorite poems, stories, or speeches. Steve found summaries of the military units stationed there from 1872 to 1877, the general fort activities, and the slang language of soldiers.

Photograph by Susan C. Reneau.

The cavalry barracks at Fort Laramie were constructed in 1874 by soldiers stationed at the post. George was listed as one of those men who worked on construction projects at the fort. Today, the barracks are fully restored and contain many uniforms and furniture from 1876.

Photograph by Susan C. Reneau.

Rock outcrops like the ones shown here dot the landscape outside Fort Laramie. George S. Howard mentions unusual rock formations in his diary.

Photograph by John Reneau.

Wagon ruts in the sandstone near Fort Laramie are a silent testimonial to the efforts of the settlers who traveled the Oregon Trail. George S. Howard was one of many cavalry soldiers who guided settlers west.

Register Cliffs near Fort Laramie contain the signatures of settlers who carved their names in the rock. Four hours were spent looking for George's signature or initials, but none were found.

Photograph by John Reneau.

Steve introduced us by telephone to the fort curator and historian of Fort Robinson Museum near Crawford, Nebraska, Thomas R. Buecker, who provided additional information to me regarding the death of Lt. Robinson, the namesake of the fort where Moccasin Joe was stationed in the early 1870s.

Louise Samson, curator of Fort Laramie, identified curious comments and references in the diary and researched the fort library materials for us. She recognized George's comments about the Indians based upon a poem composed by Alexander Pope called, "Essay on Man." Some of Louise's ancestors had settled in the area in the late 1800s and early 1900s. Fullmer's family were also long-time residents of the area.

A fascinating experience for me occurred when Louise recognized the name of one of George's girlfriends who was listed in his diary as that of her great grandmother, Elizabeth "Lizzie" Stevens. George and Lizzie dated for many months from 1875 to 1877 while he was stationed at Fort Sanders near Laramie City. They even planned to marry. In one of George's entries, he says they did marry even though in reality, this marriage never took place. One of his final entries in the 257-page diary was the mention that his relationship with Lizzie had ended.

Although Louise felt sure this was not the same woman, I could not help but wonder. Maybe Moccasin Joe and Louise's great grandmother had known each other. Very few women lived in the West before Wyoming was a state and even fewer women would have the same name. Who knows the truth?

With the help of Louise and Steve, I uncovered information about the library holdings at the fort which may have been used by George to wile away the hours. George loved to read and practice his handwriting and copied portions of speeches, stories, and poems into his diary. John and I imagined that George found his reading material from the fort library.

His daughter said he loved to take his diary with him and read the poems as a traveling library when he was in the field. He often copied favorite poems *(The Raven, The Ride of Paul Revere)* so he would always have something to read and enjoy as he waited for a commanding officer to relocate an encampment on the Western Plains. I found modern reproductions of favorite poems written in the diary, and his versions are close matches.

I closed my eyes and imagined George sitting by the window of the fort's library turning the pages of a magazine or a book. The library at Fort Laramie contained such popular magazines as *Harper's Weekly, Cincinnati Inquirer Weekly, Cheyenne Leader, Frank Leslie's Illustrated Newspaper, Detroit Free Press, Illustrated London News* and *St. Louis Globe Democrat*. Soldiers were free to check out books, magazines, and newspapers.

By 1888 when the entire library collection was transferred to Fort Robinson, the librarian wrote, "It has not been possible to ascertain the date when the post library was established. There were on hand in the Post Library January 1, 1887 Five hundred and eighteen (518) books, and on January 1, 1888, Five hundred and seventy eight (578) books. Additions since January 1, 1888 seven (7) volumes."

George's daughter said he often read by the river and relished his ability to use beautiful penmanship. Several entries in George's diary were done in pencil, a new invention in 1872, and George comments that he can get rid of unwanted writings with a flick of the wrist. John and I were struck with the pulse of life in the fort and the methods George used to pass away the hours.

Before leaving Fort Laramie, John and I walked into the fort's restored trader's store that was first built in 1849. The trader's store looks as it did in 1872 when George would have purchased writing materials, rope, medicine, and other supplies not provided by skimpy Army rations. This store may have been where George purchased his ledger book that became his diary. An entry in the store's sale book for 1872 shows that a ledger book and writing utensils were purchased by a customer. Could this be the purchase George made when he arrived at Fort Laramie on November 1, 1872? Isn't it fun to imagine that it was?

John and I viewed buffalo, fox, and deer pelts hanging on the walls; knives, soap, tools, and canned goods stashed in glass-covered display boxes; and other items George may have purchased at inflated prices to supplement his meager life. The floor boards creaked, and the musty aroma of aging wood greeted our nostrils as we examined the items displayed for sale.

We walked into the summer light and left for Register Cliffs west of the post using our metal horse. The trip took us less than a half hour. When George led wagon and lumber trains past those same cliffs, the trip took half a day. We searched for his signature on the sandstone outcroppings, but found nothing. Many of the names on the cliffs from the 1800s were obliterated by modern graffiti. A slight drizzle, followed by a cloudburst, drenched us as we stood against the cliffs to examine the names etched there since the 1840s when settlers first started trudging along the Oregon Trail. John was impressed to see the ruts of the wagon wheels still visible on the ground near the cliffs and imaged George riding his horse beside the wagons, calling to the settlers to hurry along.

We left Register Cliffs in the late afternoon of the second day of our journey and reached northwestern Wyoming seven hours later, late at night. George spent the better part of two weeks traveling this same trail to this fertile region of the West on horseback. John and I entered the Wind River Canyon south of present-day Thermopolis. We crossed, in our steel and plastic horse, the same creeks and rivers George forded as he searched for antelope, elk, and deer. Owl Creek, Buffalo Creek, Cottonwood Creek—ribbons of life for rugged landscapes—passed beneath us. Outcroppings of rock beside the road dated to 600 million years ago. We followed the Bozeman Trail past present day Douglas, Wyoming, and up into the southern reaches of Yellowstone National Park. The next morning, John hiked to the river bottom on Wind Canyon and gazed up the rugged cliffs as young Moccasin Joe would have gazed in 1873 when he went on a hunting expedition with his unnamed friend, referred to in the diary only as "Pard"— short for partner.

At the end of a dirt road off present-day Route 291 just outside of Cody, Wyoming, we jumped and climbed on top of scattered boulders along the Shoshone River in the exact area where George climbed more than 100 years before. We spent a day driving and hiking far back into grizzly country, and followed the Shoshone River past Castle Rock between the Carter and Absaroka mountain ranges. Our frequent companion was the occasional hawk or butterfly. As we drove deeper into grizzly country, we passed cattle ranches—ranches that did not come into existence until the 1890s, years after George rode through the area hunting for elk and deer. Huge granite boulders lumped together at the base of mountain cliffs in vacant riverbeds.

We picked our way upwards toward the summit of unknown mountain peaks until my motherly instincts told me we were too close to the homes of grizzly and returned to our metal horse. My son and I realized that as we looked up into the mountain canyons we were gazing upon the same rocks and indigo blue sky George had gazed upon almost 120 years before. We ended our day by returning to the comfort of the Irma Hotel, a cozy two-story hotel established by William "Buffalo Bill" Cody on November 1, 1902, in honor of his youngest daughter, Irma. Cody had established his ranch in 1899 near present-day Cody, almost thirty years after George had walked the same riverbeds.

The orange sun was setting as we reached Cody and drove into Yellowstone National Park for an evening of dining at the Old Faithful Inn, an elegant hotel that was built in 1904. We discussed how lonely George must have felt sleeping among the stars and shivering in the cold. And yet, we also imagined this young man found a certain peacefulness about camping in the wild. George wasn't bothered by honking horns and screaming children in Yellowstone, that was for sure, John said.

We sat beside a huge stone fireplace and dined on grilled trout. George, we imagined, also enjoyed trout grilled across a campfire somewhere in the Carter Mountains. George never reached Old Faithful Geyser that we viewed from the Old Faithful Inn balcony. He did come upon six grizzly just south of Cody and abandoned a horse-load of deer to avoid confrontation. After several trips to this rugged region he and his friend returned to Fort Laramie and Fort Sanders. They followed portions of the Bozeman Trail we followed as we intersected creeks and hillsides. We followed his path as closely as we could with the aid of an interstate highway. We drove and hiked through the Big Horn River Basin, past the present-day hamlets of Buffalo and Orpha that lie directly on the Bozeman Trail. I stopped for a candy bar and soda for John at Powder River, which had been a stagecoach stop one hundred years before, but nonexistent when George rode through the area.

We followed the Oregon Trail from Casper, Wyoming, back to Fort Laramie after first hiking the grounds of Fort Fetterman outside present-day Douglas. Casper and Douglas did not become towns until the 1880s. John commented that he could understand why George wrote so much poetry. He said the land was so expansive, thought-provoking, and quiet. Poetry was the only way to capture the freedom and spirit of the land. Days on end of riding in a hard saddle could become boring, John thought, so writing poetry was a way to escape the monotony.

We drove 214 miles south from Cody to Casper and passed only a handful of people, cars, trucks, and houses. In the early 1870s, the only company George would have had was his diary and the occasional Sioux or Shoshone hunter. We stopped for a taco and gas in Casper and felt out of place in the modern world as we read from the pages of George's diary describing the vastness of the Wyoming countryside where Casper would eventually develop.

Visiting Fort Fetterman was another step back into time. The fort, located less than 60 miles southwest from present-day Casper, was established in 1867. George and hundreds of men gathered at the fort in 1876 for the start of the Big Horn Expedition. George mentioned the quantity of jackrabbits and butterflies as a delightful source of entertainment. While visiting the fort ruins, John spent an hour chasing an abundant supply of jackrabbits and butterflies that were probably the great, great, great, great grandchildren of the creatures George chased, John figured. The curator of Fort Fetterman, Stanley Lass, age 89, is the grandson of the fort's blacksmith, Charles "Charlie" Rice. Charlie may have worked and lived at the fort when George was there. Stanley wasn't sure how long his grandfather was at Fort Fetterman. As a cavalry scout, George would have known the blacksmith. John and I wondered if Moccasin Joe and Charlie had worked together. We were charmed by Stanley's tales of fort activity and his grandfather's job. We knew he was proud of his heritage and his connection with Fort Fetterman. We enjoyed the thought that our man knew his grandfather. As George waited for a new shoe to be fitted on his horse, we imagined him passing the time with Charlie talking about weather conditions, hunting and fishing, and fort activity.

As we stood overlooking the winding river valley atop the fort's bluff, we imagined thousands of white canvas tents lining the Platte River at the start of the Big Horn Expedition. Sheep bleated their discontent at our arrival as we returned to our steel horse to travel back to Fort Laramie. The day at Fort Fetterman had flooded our senses with the sounds and movements George would have experienced in 1876.

We returned to Fort Laramie in a few hours after first stopping in Douglas—a town established in 1886. George spent three to four days making the same 90-mile journey downriver to Fort Laramie. John and I visited the Wyoming Pioneer Museum in Douglas less than ten miles south of Fort Fetterman and spoke with Arleen Ernst, curator of the museum; Claudia Goodin, assistant curator; and Edna Davies, whose family settled in the Douglas area in the late 1880s, ten years after George passed through the area on his way to Yellowstone. We viewed wagons, kitchen utensils, clothing, photographs, and other common household items from the 1880s when the town began. We were struck with how basic and primitive George's existence would have been in 1872 in comparison to the settlers who came less than twenty years later. Very little on display in the museum related to George's life.

George explored rivers, creeks, and canyons in Wyoming and reached southern Montana as far north as the junction of the Little Big Horn and Big Horn Rivers. In his exploration of southeastern Montana, he rode along the Rosebud, Deer, Tongue, Mizpah, and Powder Rivers to the eastern end of present-day South Dakota. Montana remained a territory until 1889 when it joined the United States. South Dakota was a territory until 1890 when it became a state.

He rode beside and fished in the Belle Fourche River, and enjoyed the wildness of the gold towns of Deadwood, Custer City, and Crook City. As we traveled past these river landmarks and into the area where George Armstrong Custer met his doom in June of 1876, we imagined how this New England man must have felt as he explored uncharted and barren land that was uninhabited by white men and women.

When my three sons viewed the site of the Battle of the Little Big Horn in September of 1992, we imagined hearing the screams and gun shots as men on both sides fell. My sons spent more than two hours roaming the golden-grassed hillsides and ridges that housed thousands of Sioux and Cheyenne in 1876. They pretended to reenact the battle with my husband as I negotiated a sales contract with realtors on our house in Washington, D.C., via an 800 number in a pay phone booth to the back of the battle's museum and display room.

We drove past the spot where George camped south of the battle site on June 24, 1876, and where he observed smoke rising from the ridges that became the battle site the next day. He mentions the smoke in his diary, but does not know he witnessed the battle until a week later. Except for a few stores and a casino, the land around the battlefield remains undeveloped today.

My husband, sons, and I drove past Deadwood, Fort Phil Kearny, Fort Reno and numerous rivers and creeks as we headed north into Montana and a new life away from the violent dangers and excessive human population of Washington, D.C. As we drove deeper into the Montana vastness, we commented that George would have felt the same way as he left behind the comforts and challenges of his life in the East. We stopped for an afternoon of exploration in the Black Hills of South Dakota and took our sons to Mount Rushmore—a monument non-existent until the mid 20th century—and watered our metal horse that became overheated on the steep climb down the mountain. I wondered how many times in a day George must have had to pause to water his steed as he transversed the riverbeds and canyons of the Black Hills. I vowed that I would return to the Black Hills with my sons to explore the canyons again.

George scouted for miners in the Black Hills; guided settlers and loggers past Laramie Peak in Wyoming; hunted for elk and deer throughout Montana, Wyoming, and the Dakotas; whooped it up in Deadwood; and fought for his life in numerous battles. He witnessed some of the last massive herds of wild buffalo migrating across the grassy Plains north of Laramie and saw a sundance. It was in the Black Hills that he fought in the Battle of Slim Buttes and ate horse and mule meat along Owl Creek because he was starving.

George rode as far as Omaha, Nebraska, and returned again to Fort Laramie and Fort Sanders to end his five-year enlistment. We passed through the same towns and rivers as we migrated to Montana from Washington, D.C. What took George five years of horseback riding to complete his journey, took us less than two weeks.

What struck us was the distance George traveled by himself or with a handful of soldiers and Indians. When our metal horse overheated, a highway patrolman arrived within fifteen minutes to offer aid. George was alone to fend for himself using all his resources for survival. Fear was not in his vocabulary; loneliness and endurance were. He did what was needed to survive and in the process developed a respect for the Sioux, Shoshone, and Cheyenne.

George did not understand why peaceful Indian villages, filled with old men, women, and children, had to endure the torturous attacks of marauding soldiers armed with rifles. He did not understand why two cultures were at odds with each other and why so many soldiers on both sides died. He was torn by the violence of battles that killed his white friends, and he grieved for the wasted lives on both sides. To the Army, the Native American tribes were the enemy, and George felt the pang of conflict when he recorded battles and deaths on the Plains and composed his poetry and prose to preserve his feelings.

Moccasin Joe continued to feel this conflict long after leaving the West, his daughter said. She said her father recognized that the Cheyenne, Sioux, and Shoshone had the same human needs and desires of the white men, but their way of life was in direct conflict with the expansionist ways of white settlers and miners who saw an economic future in the West that was not available in the crowded East. In the end, the buffalo hunters, miners, settlers, and soldiers dominated the Western landscape that had been for thousands of years the property of the Gods. By the close of the 1870s, the sacred Indian hunting grounds and pasturelands were dominated by white men and women. The battles were coming to an end and many proud warriors on both sides lay dead.

Walking in the footsteps of Moccasin Joe offered me and my 20th century family the opportunity to empathize with another young man from another century in America's history. The trips we took through Wyoming, Montana, Nebraska, and South Dakota in 1990 and 1992 provided the proper perspective for understanding where the diary fits in the fabric of American history. I missed this perspective by only reading microfilm at the National Archives in Washington, D.C.

The diary of George S. Howard provides a window into the soul of an enlisted man who felt his experiences were worth recording. My husband, sons and I were grateful he took the time to record the landmarks he crossed so we could follow in his footsteps 120 years later. John felt a oneness, a connection, with another young man from another century who experienced the Western wilderness for the first time after living in the comforts of eastern civilization. Like his great, great, great, great uncle before him, John was struck with the similarities in George's life to his. Both were young men living in the East who traveled West to find a new life.

George seemed a quiet, reflective type to us. His writings captured the ruggedness of the environment in which he lived. As John and I read and transcribed the diary pages, George's massive hulk hovered over our shoulders. My son felt the same spirit as he read the diary entries on journeys to the Wind River Canyon, Big Panther Mountain, Goose Creek, and the Little Big Horn. He felt a kinship with another young man from another time who seemed to have the same kinds of emotions and reactions to situations that John imagined he would have had if he had been a scout in Wyoming and Montana in 1872.

George was tormented by a head injury and died violently, but his diary reflects a contemplative spirit who wanted to be loved by everyone. His parting wish in his diary was the hope that the readers of his book would think he was not half bad. He wasn't.

Photograph courtesy of National Archives.

Rain-in-the-Face, a Hunkpapa Sioux, was one of one of the chiefs at the Battle of Rosebud and fought at the Battle of Little Big Horn one week later in June 1876. Information on the back of this photograph in the National Archives indicates he may have been the Indian to kill Col. Custer.

Annotated Bibliography

[The following reference materials provided the background to understand George S. Howard's diary. From January of 1977 to January of 1994, I read everything I could get my hands on that explained the historic backdrop of this most violent and tragic period in American history.

My research has ended for this book, but I will always crave new books and magazine articles about this period because of George's diary.

This bibliography only includes the newspaper articles, books, documents, and other printed materials that were extensively used in my effort to understand Moccasin Joe.

Without these books, newspapers, pamphlets, and National Archives' records, the diary would not have made much sense. The reference materials are listed alphabetically by author, if an author exists, or by title.

Original newspaper articles were found in the Library of Congress and the Fitchburg, Massachusetts, library. Books and pamphlets about trains and train injuries of the mid-1800s were located at the Association of American Railroads (AAR) library. For more information about how the research was conducted using these materials, read Chapter One and Six of this book.]

————. "Accident on the Vermont and Massachusetts Railroad," *Boston Journal*, Boston, Mass., Monday morning edition, June 20, 1870, page 2.

Late and brief account of serious train accident when George S. Howard was injured with fractured skull on June 16, 1870.

Bordeaux, William J. *Sitting Bull, Tanka-Iyotaka*. Custer Ephemera Society, Grand Rapids, Mich. 1974.

A tender and accurate portrayal of one of the most famous Sioux Indian chiefs of the 1870s whom George S. Howard knew as a medicine man. Provided excellent understanding of Sitting Bull and his time period.

Bouknight, Marie, and Robert Gruber. *Guide to Records in the Military Archives Division Pertaining to Indian-White Relations*. National Archives, Government Printing Office, Wash., D.C. 1977.

Helpful guide to locate microfilm in the National Archives related to the Indian War period of Western history. This booklet helped me find military personnel files, regimental reports, and other original materials that related to George's activities in the West.

Bourke, Capt. John G. *On the Border with Crook*. Charles Scribner's Sons, New York, N.Y. 1891.

Little Big Man was a subchief of the Oglala Sioux under Crazy Horse.

Bourke rode with Gen. Crook throughout the general's career in the West and recorded those events in his daily diary. Of special interest are Chapters 14 to 24, which record Bourke's impressions of events throughout the Indian War period in Wyoming, Montana, and the Dakota Territories. His entries match the entries of George Howard, except Bourke's information is from the perspective of an officer. A reprint of this original diary is available through Time-Life Books.

————. "Broken Bridge: Railway Accident at Athol," *Boston Daily Advertiser*, Boston, Mass. Friday morning edition, June 17, 1870, Front Page.

One of first detailed accounts of serious railroad accident on June 16, 1870, involving George S. Howard who received a fractured skull. Complete article reproduced in Chapter Two of the book.

Bryan, Gene, Clyde Douglass, and Elayne Wallis. *Wyoming: 1890 to 1990*. Wyoming Travel Commission, Cheyenne, Wyo. 1990.

Commemorative book pictures the colorful history and current attractions of Wyoming in its centennial year as a state. Historical and modern photographs illustrate the events of this state. This book and other materials were given to me by U.S. Senator Alan Simpson (R-Wyo.) when I visited his offices in 1990 to prepare for my trip to his state. His assistant Elizabeth Shaw helped make arrangements for me to visit the Buffalo Bill Historical Center in Cody, Wyo., research library in 1990.

Buffalo Chamber of Commerce. *Buffalo, Wyoming*. Buffalo Chamber of Commerce and Wyoming Travel Commission, Buffalo, Wyo. 1990.

Excellent booklet summarizing historic sites and significance of this Western town located on the Bozeman Trail and in the Big Horn Mountain region where George S. Howard roamed for five years. The forts of Reno, McKinney, Phil Kearny, and Fetterman Monument located near town. The town did not exist in early 1870s, but the forts were well known to George.

————. "Coroner's Inquest," *Fitchburg Sentinel*, Fitchburg, Mass., Saturday edition, July 2, 1870, page 2.

Complete testimony of Coroner Miller's at inquest regarding June 16, 1870, train accident involving George S. Howard. The extent of George's injury and treatment was detailed and included in Chapter One of this book.

Crofutt, George A. *Crofutt's New Overland Tourist and Pacific Coast Guide*. Overland Publishing Company, Chicago, Ill. 1872, 1873, 1874, 1875, 1876, 1877, and 1878. Published annually throughout 1800s.

Original Crofutt's travel guide series to the Western states found in the Association of American Railroads (AAR) library in Wash., D.C. Contains 1,200 descriptions of cities;

Dull Knife (sitting), a chief of the Cheyenne at the Battle of the Little Big Horn, and Little Wolf (standing) were mentioned in George's diary. This studio portrait was taken prior to 1877 at the time George was roaming the West.

towns; villages; train stations; government forts and camps; mountains; lakes; rivers; sulfur, soda, and hot springs; scenery; watering places; and summer resorts in Nebraska, Wyoming, Colorado, Utah, Montana, Idaho, Nevada, California, and Arizona. Official guide book for travelers using Union, Central, and Southern Pacific Railroad Companies' trains, stages, and water boats. Valuable research tool used in understanding George's writings.

Crook, Gen. George. *General George Crook: His Autobiography.* Edited by Martin F. Schmitt. University of Oklahoma Press, Norman, Okla. 1960.

Complete life story written by Gen. George Crook with special emphasis upon his military career.

Davenport, Reuben Briggs. "The Skirmish at Tongue River Heights," *New York Herald*, New York, N.Y. June 16, 1876.

The exact article Davenport filed contained extensive detail not mentioned by George in his diary since George was in the battle. The microfilmed copy of the article is found in the Library of Congress and an excellent reproduction of it is in Jerome A. Greene's book, Battles and Skirmishes of the Great Sioux War, 1876–1877: The Military View.

_____. "Death of George S. Howard," *Fitchburg Sentinel*, Fitchburg, Mass., January 21, 1887, page 3.

Announcement of George S. Howard's death after the shooting January 18, 1887, in the Fitchburg railroad yards.

_____. "Death of the Late George S. Howard, The Autopsy Report," and "Communication with Community about the Late George S. Howard," *Fitchburg Sentinel*, Fitchburg, Mass., January 22, 1887, page 3.

Complete autopsy report of George S. Howard after shooting on January 18, 1887. This report is reproduced in Chapter Two of this book.

Dixon, E. H. "Trephining in Neuralgia of the Cranium," *Boston Surgical and Medical Journal.* Daniel Clapp Co., Boston, Mass., 1847.

Case study of Mrs. Bishop of Easton, Pa., who had trephining performed June 18, 1846, after her skull was crushed 17 years prior to the operation. After operation, all unpleasant symptoms vanished. Original journal found in the fabulous research library of the American Association of Railroads in Wash., D.C.

Dublin Medical Press and Circular. "Indications for Trephining," *Boston Medical and Surgical Journal.* Daniel Clapp, Boston, Mass., April 28, 1870, page 324.

Article from Dublin Medical Press and Circular *about the use of trephining when a patient has fractures of the skull and mechanical lesions of the head that produce compression*

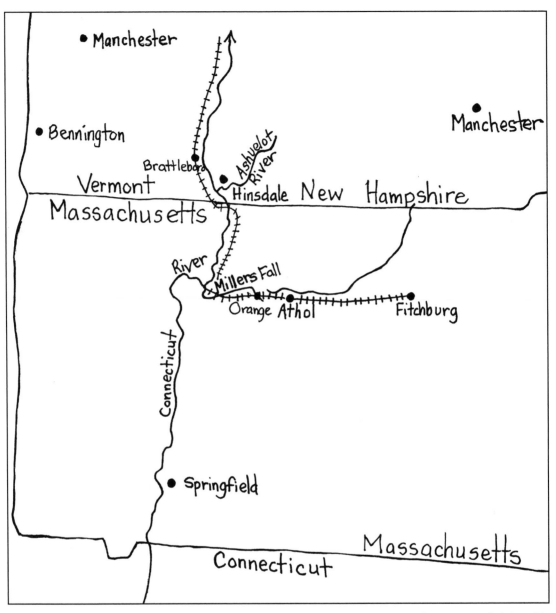

A map of the railroads of the Connecticut Valley in 1870 when George S. Howard was seriously injured in a train accident on the Vermont and Massachusetts Railroad near Athol, Massachusetts.

of the brain. Detailed description of the medical procedure. This was the procedure performed on George in 1870 when a metal plate was inserted into his skull. A description of this procedure as described in the Dublin Medical Press and Circular is reproduced in Chapter One.

──────. "Fatal Railroad Disaster," *The Baltimore Sun*, Baltimore, Md., Friday morning edition, June 17, 1870, Front Page.

Small article edited from Boston newspapers detailing serious train accident at Athol, Mass., that involved George S. Howard.

Fleming, Paula Richardson, and Judith Luskey. *The North American Indians in Early Photographs*. Dorset Press, New York, N.Y. 1986.

Reproductions of most of the famous Indian chiefs and Indian lifestyle photographs from the 19th century with detailed photo captions and historical annotations. This book was a source of information about the Indians who George knew, respected, and feared.

Frazer, Robert W. *Forts of the West*. University of Oklahoma Press, Norman, Okla. 1965, 1972.

Descriptions of military forts and posts west of the Mississippi River provide readers clear understanding of Western geography and fort locations. Forts are listed under the 23 states where they are located. Of special help are descriptions and map locations of forts in Wyoming, Montana, Nebraska, and South Dakota where George S. Howard was stationed.

Gray, John S. *Centennial Campaign: The Sioux War of 1876*. Foreword by Robert M. Utley. University of Oklahoma Press, Norman and London. 1976.

The author captures the spirit of the conflicts during the 1876 Indian Wars and adds color to this period of Western history with his analysis of the situation. Maps of the Sioux War Country, the Crook-Reynolds Powder River Campaign, Terry's march down the Powder River, and Crook's Rosebud Campaign were especially helpful as they related to George S. Howard's diary entries.

Greene, Jerome A. *Battles and Skirmishes of the Great Sioux War, 1876–1877: The Military View*. University of Oklahoma Press, Norman and London. 1993.

I had copied newspaper articles from the Library of Congress and National Archives documents sections using microfilm copying machines, but the quality of reproduction was not good. I had poured over original personal files of George's commanding officers, sometimes not knowing which bits of information were important and which were not. This book provided a clear reproduction of many of the original documents I had struggled to read in the National Archives since 1977. Jerome does a wonderful job introducing each article so the reader understands where the author of the article fits in the historic perspective of things.

The destruction of the extensive bison herds in the 1870s brought an end to the Native American way of life. George S. Howard mentions bison hunts throughout his diary and said the herds were gone from the Laramie Plains when he arrived at Fort Sanders in 1874. This photograph was taken in 1872.

Greene, Jerome A. *Slim Buttes, 1876: An Episode of the Great Sioux War.* University of Oklahoma Press, Norman and London. 1982.

Details the Big Horn and Yellowstone Expeditions, the soldier's life on the campaign trail, and official reports of the commanding officers involved with the battle. Of special interest was the chapter titled, "Hunger and Mud," which detailed the sacrifice the Western soldier endured during the campaigns.

Hallock, Morris G., Publisher. *Old West Train Vacation Guide: The Official Publication of the Old West Trail.* Old West Trail, Rapid City, S.D. 1990.

Provides brief descriptions of historical events and modern attractions in the states of Montana, North and South Dakota, Wyoming, and Nebraska where George S. Howard roamed. Many of the attractions listed were places George visited and lived.

Hamilton, Allan McLane, M.D. *Railway and Other Accidents with Relation to Injury and Disease of the Nervous System: A Book for Court Use.* William Wood and Co., New York, N.Y. 1902.

Extensive medical book for physicians and attorneys dealing with railroad accident victims. Detailed descriptions of injuries, case studies, treatments, and causes of such injuries. Of special interest was Chapter 3 titled, "Injuries of the Cranium and Its Contents," where the author discusses fractured skulls and the general symptoms of brain disease and injury caused from trauma to the skull. Lengthy discussion of traumatic insanity, which George experienced after returning to New England from the West. Original book found in the AAR research library.

Hart, Herbert M. *Old Forts of the Northwest.* Illustrations by Paul J. Hartle. Superior Publishing Company. 1990.

Illustrations of Western forts identified and described. Of special interest is an 1875 pen-and-ink illustration of Fort Sanders as George S. Howard would have seen it while stationed there.

Hedren, Paul L. *Fort Laramie in 1876: Chronicle of a Frontier Post at War.* University of Oklahoma Press, Lincoln, Neb., and London, England. 1988.

This valuable reference book contains chapters on Fort Laramie's role during the Indian Wars of 1876 and details about the movement of Indians and troops from January 1876 to January 1877. Information in the book followed the entries of George S. Howard's diary and helped to clarify his passages.

Hedren, Paul L. *With Crook in the Black Hills.* Photographs by Stanley J. Morrow. Pruett Publishing Company, Boulder, Colo. 1985.

Sitting Bear, a Kiowa chief, is mentioned in George S. Howard's diary. This photograph was taken by William S. Soule.

The photographs of and commentary about Stanley J. Morrow provide insight into the Western history recorded by one of the most famous photographers of the 1870s. Many of Morrow's photographs recorded the Big Horn Expedition, Starvation March, and other key events of 1876 which George Howard described in his five-year diary.

Herrick, Clinton B., M.D. "Railroad Surgery," *Medical Society of New York Transactions.* New York, N.Y. 1891.

Surgeon from Troy, N.Y., discusses variety of railroad accidents and types of treatment, including the use of trephining. Case studies examined. Fascinating accounts of 19th century medical practices. Original book found in the AAR research library. Focused on pages 325 to 331 of publication.

————. *Historic Forts of the Old West.* Office of the Chief, Public Affairs, Sixth United States Army, Presidio of San Francisco, Calif. 1976.

A map in this fold-out pamphlet shows the location of some Western forts in Montana, Nebraska, Nevada, New Mexico, North Dakota, Oregon, South Dakota, Utah, Washington, and Wyoming, to celebrate the bicentennial of the United States.

Howard, George S. "Extracts from a Diary," *Winners of the West*, Vol. XIV, No. 3. National Indian War Veterans U.S.A., St. Joseph, Mo. 1937.

Front-page extract of a few pages of George's diary printed in the official bulletin of the National Indian War Veterans and published in the interest of the survivors of Indian Wars and the Old Army of the Plains. Extract probably given to newspaper by Grace Howard Porter, who mentioned to me that she showed the original diary to government officials many years ago. The Time-Life book, The Soldiers, *quotes the diary from this printed version.*

————. "Howard-Connor Case: Testimony at the Inquest," *Fitchburg Sentinel*, Fitchburg, Mass., Jan. 25, 1887, page 3.
————. "Howard-Connor Case," *Fitchburg Sentinel*, Fitchburg, Mass., Jan. 27, 1887, page 3.
————. "Howard-Connor Case," *Fitchburg Sentinel*, Fitchburg, Mass., Jan. 28, 1887, page 3.

Three newspaper accounts record the complete testimony at trial of Officer Michael M. Connor who shot George S. Howard in the neck on January 18, 1887. George died from the injuries on January 21, 1887, at age 36, less than ten years after he left Fort Sanders, Wyo. as a cavalry scout.

Hutton, Paul Andrew, Editor. *Soldiers West: Biographies from the Military Frontier.* Introduction by Robert M. Utley. University of Nebraska Press, Lincoln, Neb. 1987.

Of special help were the short biographies of Gen. Philip H. Sheridan, Gen. George Crook, Col. George Armstrong Custer, Lt. John G. Bourke, and Capt. Charles King who played important roles in the life of George S. Howard, directly or indirectly.

———. "Late Railroad Tragedy," *Fitchburg Sentinel*, Fitchburg, Mass., Saturday edition, June 25, 1870, page 3.

Additional information about a serious train accident near Fitchburg at Athol, Mass., involving George S. Howard on June 16, 1870.

———. "Inquest," *Fitchburg Sentinel*, Fitchburg, Mass., January 26, 1887, page 3.

Testimony of Dr. Miller who performed autopsy on George S. Howard, January 22, 1887. The complete autopsy is reproduced in Chapter Two of this book.

———. "Inquest into the Death of George S. Howard," *Fitchburg Sentinel*, Fitchburg, Mass., January 24, 1887, page 3.

Announcement of names of people who were called to testify at the trial of Police Officer Michael M. Connor who shot George S. Howard January 18, 1887. Beginning testimony at trial.

Kellogg, A. N. *Railroad Gazette: A Journal of Transportation*. A. N. Kellogg, Chicago, Ill., and New York, N.Y. 1870, 1886, 1887.

Original quarterly journals on transportation published in the 19th century found in the AAR research library. Focus on an article written June 18, 1870, on compensation for railway accidents. George's train accident occurred June 16, 1870. Also focused on railway schedules and financial reports of Fitchburg Railroad, January 1886 and 1887. George was shot in the Fitchburg Railroad yard on January 18, 1887. The February 25, 1887, issue lists all January accidents, but not by name, location, or date. Since this was a shooting, and not a mechanical accident, George's incident was not reported in the journal.

King, Capt. Charles. *Campaigning with Crook*. Introduction by Don Russell. University of Oklahoma Press, Norman, Okla. 1964.

As acting regimental adjutant during the Sioux Campaign of 1876, King records his impressions and observations of historic events taking place in 1876. The book contains King's daily entries of events as they happened and provides an excellent backdrop for George S. Howard's writings.

Knight, Oliver. *Following the Indian Wars*. University of Oklahoma Press, Norman, Okla. 1960.

Details events of 19th century Indian conflicts and white expansion. Information used to understand comments by George.

Larrey, Baron. "Trephining," *Boston Medical and Surgical Journal*. Boston, Mass., September 9, 1869.

Caution from this surgeon to the readers regarding the use of trephining due to the serious nature of the operation. George had this procedure performed on him in 1870.

Lavender, David. *Fort Laramie and the Changing Frontier.* Division of Publications, National Park Service, U.S. Department of Interior, Wash., D.C. 1983.

A vivid description of every part of the most famous and active Western fort and the life of an average Western recruit stationed there from its beginnings in 1834 to its abandonment in the spring of 1890 is contained in this official National Park Service handbook. Excellent map showing the entire region surrounding Fort Laramie from Nebraska to the western reaches of Wyoming, north to Montana, and south to Colorado.

————. "Man Shot by Officer M. Connor," *Fitchburg Sentinel*, Fitchburg, Mass., January 18, 1887, page 3.

First article detailing how George S. Howard was shot. Exact reproduction of article is in Chapter Two of this book.

Mangum, Neil C. *Battle of the Rosebud: Prelude to the Little Big Horn.* Upton & Sons, El Segundo, Calif. 1987.

Excellent background information on Indian War period. Special interest on chapters regarding the Battle of Powder River, the Big Horn and Yellowstone Expeditions, trout fishing by soldiers, and cavalry life.

Manley, Thomas H., Ph.D., M.D. "On the Passing of the Trephine," *Boston Medical and Surgical Journal.* Boston, Mass. October 31, 1901, page 496.

Detailed description of the use of the medical instrument, the trephine, and how the instrument "has no place at the present time in the therapy of cranial surgery." This instrument was used on George when his skull was crushed in the 1870 train accident.

Marshall, S. L. A. *Crimsoned Prairie: The Indian Wars.* Scribner Book Companies, Inc. and Da Capo Press, New York, N.Y. 1972.

Chronicles the Western events of the white man's expansion and Indian battles. Of special interest are the maps showing the Bozeman Trail, Fort Phil Kearny, and movements of the Sioux Expedition of 1876 which helped pinpoint the movements of George S. Howard at the time.

McCleary, Edythe, Editor. *Montana's Custer Country.* Custer Country, Inc. 1990.

The rivers of Yellowstone, Powder River, Big Horn, Little Big Horn, and Tongue are described as well as the historic events that took place along them. Many of the events described in this book involved the activities of George S. Howard.

Crow King, wearing Maj. Brotherton's coat in this photograph, led a band of Sioux in a charge on Col. Custer's men on June 25, 1876. Maj, Brotherton permitted Crow King to keep his horse when Indian horses were confiscated after the Battle of Little Big Horn. George S. Howard mentions him in his diary.

Mills, Anson. *My Story.* Byron S. Adams, editor. Wash., D.C. 1918.

Capt. Mills relates his side of Western history in his autobiography. He was one of many commanding officers over George S. Howard.

National Archives. *Compiled Records Showing Service of Military Units in Volunteer Union Organizations, 1860–1865.* Microfilm M594.

Focus on George S. Howard's enlistment as private (drummer boy) from 1861 to 1863. Found his enlistment information, but details were very sketchy. I reviewed microfilm of Union soldiers from 1979 to 1991 to locate George's file. George's file was mixed up with his brother's because George used his brother's birthday to become a drummer boy at age 11 years.

National Archives. *Correspondence of the Office of Indian Affairs and Related Records.* National Archives, Wash., D.C., 1824–1880. Microfilm roll M18 (26 rolls).

Rolls of microfilm contain the name of letter writer, date of letter, date received (beginning in April 1834), place where written, summary of contents, where it was filed, and file number assigned each letter (starting July 1836). Focused on rolls related to 1872 to 1877. Fascinating correspondence with and about Indians.

National Archives. *Historical Information Relating to Military Posts and Other Installations.* National Archives, Wash., D.C. Microfilm roll M725.

Focus on military posts where George S. Howard was stationed from 1872 to 1877, especially the forts of Laramie, D. A. Russell, Sanders, Omaha Barracks, and Fetterman.

National Archives. *Indexes to Letters Received by the Office of Adjutant General Main Series, 1846, 1861–1889.* National Archives, Wash., D.C. Microfilm M725.

Focus on letters related to Civil War from recruits in Massachusetts and letters related to Indian Wars of 1872 to 1877. Sketchy information in these files.

National Archives. *Letters Sent by Headquarters of the Army, Main Series, 1828–1903, on Indian Affairs.* National Archives, Wash., D.C. Microfilm roll M857.

Focus on letters related to Indian affairs from 1872–1877 at forts where George S. Howard located based upon unit reports and his diary.

National Archives. *Report Books of Office of Indian Affairs, 1838–1885.* National Archives, Wash., D.C. Microfilm M348, rolls 21 to 29 (September 7, 1871 to December 29, 1877).

Focus on reports related to Indian Wars of 1872–1877 in areas where George S. Howard was stationed and participated in events.

Soldiers cinch a load of flour on a pack mule during the Starvation March or Horsemeat March of 1876. This was one of 31 stereoscopic photographs by Stanley J. Morrow depicting the Big Horn Expedition. George's concern for good grazing lands is mentioned throughout his diary.

National Archives. *Returns from Regular Army Cavalry Regiments, 1833–1916.* National Archives and Records Service, General Services Administration, Wash., D.C. Microfilm M744, roll 19.

Focus on Company E, 2nd Cavalry unit returns filed by commanding officers. Provided details of George S. Howard's official assignments during his five-year enlistment. George listed throughout returns. Official assignments relate to his diary writings. Most helpful of all microfilmed records. So helpful, in fact, I purchased a copy of the roll.

National Archives. *Returns from U.S. Military Posts, 1800–1916.* National Archives and Records Service, General Services Administration, Wash., D.C. Microfilm M617, rolls 596, 1094, 1050, 1051, 879, 880.

Focus on returns from Western posts where George S. Howard served; specifically Fort Laramie, Camp Sheridan, Fort Fetterman, Fort D. A. Russell, Fort Sanders, Red Cloud Agency, Whetstone Agency, Omaha Barracks, and Camp G. H. Collins. Spent fourteen years reviewing reports from various post returns of the 1872–1877 time period. Full of interesting details about military life. Very helpful.

National Railway Publication Company. *Golden Spike Centennial Issue of Travelers' Official Railway Guide.* University Microfilms, A Xerox Company, Ann Arbor, Mich. 1969.

Exact reproduction of June 1869 railway guide book to commemorate completion of the first transcontinental rail route by connection of the Union Pacific and Central Pacific Railways, Promontory, Utah, May 10, 1869. Railway schedules to Cheyenne, Wyo., and other Western cities are detailed in chart form. Written descriptions of towns and sites along railroad routes. Book found in AAR library.

Nebraska Game and Parks Commission. "Fort Robinson Illustrated," *NEBRASKAland Magazine*, Lincoln, Neb. Jan./Feb. 1986. 64(1).

Noted Western historians write articles about the Red Cloud Agency days, the Indian Wars of 1874 to 1880, transition and final years of the fort, the prehistoric era, and information about Nebraska's first park.

Nevin, Peter. *The Soldiers.* Time-Life Books, New York, N.Y. 1973.

One book in a series on the Old West that chronicles the cavalry soldier during the Indian Wars, Western forts, and highlights of the Western campaign trail. Significant in this book are a brief references to George S. Howard's diary on pages 96 and 122. Excellent illustrations and photographs.

Parker, Watson. *Gold in the Black Hills.* University of Oklahoma Press, Norman, Okla. 1966.

George refers to Camp Collins in the Black Hills which Watson Parker identifies in this book as a site near the town of Custer City. George and his company camped outside of

Custer City in 1876. The 2nd Cavalry also stayed in Camp Collier which was known to soldiers as Camp at the Mouth of Red Canyon. South Dakota State Historical Society Archivist Marvene Riis uncovered the identification of these obscure camps George mentions in his prose and poetry.

Peters, Joseph P. *Indian Battles and Skirmishes on the American Frontier, 1790–1898.* Argonaut Press Ltd., New York, N.Y. 1966.

Contains records of engagements with Indians within the Military Division of the Missouri from 1868 to 1882; a chronological list of actions with Indians from January 1, 1866, to January 1891; and a compilation of Indian engagements from January 1837 to January 1866, prepared by the Historical Section, Army War College. This book was especially helpful to me when understanding George's references to battles in his diary.

———. "Police Court," *Fitchburg Sentinel*, Fitchburg, Mass., February 3, 1887, page 3.

Continued testimony of the trial of Officer Michael M. Connor who shot George S. Howard on January 18, 1887.

———. "Police Court: Manslaughter Case," *Fitchburg Sentinel*, Fitchburg, Mass., February 11, 1887, page 3.

Officer Michael M. Connor was convicted of manslaughter for shooting death of George S. Howard. Fined $5,000 by judge, and remained in jail since shooting because could not post bail of $500.

Poor, Henry V. *Manual of the Railroads of the United States for 1870–71.* H. V. & H. W. Poor, New York, NY. 1871, 1872, 1878–1887.

Books, published annually by Mr. Poor, contain full analysis of debts of railroad companies in the United States, shows their mileage, stocks, costs, traffic earnings, expenses, and organization. Focused on sections related to the Boston and Maine; Fitchburg; and Vermont and Massachusetts Railroads, which were companies on which George worked. Original books discovered at the AAR library in Wash., D.C.

Porter, John Sherman, Editor. *Moody's Manual of Investments, American and Foreign, on Railroad Securities.* Moody's Investors Service, New York, N.Y. 1940.

Focus on historic sketch of Boston and Maine Railroad that employed George from 1868 to 1872. Detailed route map shows service of railroad line in 1940.

———. "Railroad Accident!" *Fitchburg Sentinel*, Fitchburg, Mass., June 18, 1870, page 2.

First article in local newspaper regarding serious train accident on June 16, 1870, at Athol, involving George S. Howard who was a brakeman.

Ramsay, H. A., M.D. "Trephining in Apoplexy and Inflammation of the Brain," *Boston Medical and Surgical Journal.* David Clapp. Boston, Mass., April 18, 1853.

Letter to the editor of the medical journal encouraging fellow surgeons to use trephining for the relief of brain infection. Says "such a procedure is no more as serious as other brain surgeries." Article on pages 283 and 284.

Rickey, Don Jr. *Forty Miles a Day on Beans and Hay.* University of Oklahoma Press, Norman, Okla. 1963.

Excellent analysis of daily life of a Western recruit and officer. Helpful when visualizing how George S. Howard lived during his five-year enlistment. George's diary confirms living conditions reported by Rickey. George's diary is mentioned on page 329–330. The quote reads, "Second Cavalryman George S. Howard's story of the Sibley scout, wherein a detachment of soldiers barely escaped from a large party of Sioux, in July, 1876, mentions anouther such instance (of battle fatigue): 'Cornwall, of Co. D became insane from fright and suffering.'"

Roberts, Robert. *Encyclopedia of Historic Forts.* Macmillan Publishing Co., New York, N.Y. 1987.

Forts, camps, agencies, and other Old Army sites used in the 19th century throughout the West are described. The description of Camp Sheridan in present-day South Dakota was used in Chapter One of this book.

Rosa, Joseph G., and Robin May. *Buffalo Bill and His Wild West: A Pictorial Biography.* University Press of Kansas, Topeka, Kan. 1989.

Rare photographs of Buffalo Bill and other Western characters are identified and discussed. Clear biographical sketches of Cody and his friends are provided.

Schmitt, Martin F. *Fighting Indians of the West.* Scribner, New York, N.Y. 1948.

Detailed descriptions of conflicts between Indians and white settlers and soldiers during the 19th century.

Schultz, John H., Editor. *American Railroad Journal of Steam, Navigation, Commerce, Finance, Engineering, Banking, Mining, Manufacturers.* Schultz, New York, N.Y. 1870, 1871, 1872.

Focus on financial, construction, and business reports of Vermont and Massachusetts Railroad and Boston and Maine Railroad, which employed George. Very small railroad companies so very small reports. Original books found in AAR library—what a treasure.

Shaughnessy, Jim. *The Rutland Road: Green Mountain Rutland Gateway.* Howell-North Books, Berkeley, Calif. 1964.

Maj. Gen. George Crook is buried at Arlington National Cemetery outside Washington, D.C., on land that belonged to the Robert E. Lee family before the Civil War. Many Union officers were buried in Lee's backyard after the Civil War as a final insult to the Confederate general.

Capt. John G. Bourke served under Crook for fifteen years and authored the most famous daily diary of the Indian Wars. He is buried a short distance from his former superior at Arlington National Cemetery

Photograph by Jack Reneau.

Maj. Gen. Joseph J. Reynolds retired shortly after his court martial in 1877 and is buried near Capt. John G. Bourke at Arlington National Cemetery. After the Battle of Powder River, George Howard used Reynold's name as a nom de plume when signing poetry in his diary.

Paymaster Gen. Thaddeus H. Stanton is buried a short distance from Maj. Gen. Crook at Arlington National Cemetery. Stanton was chief of scouts during the Big Horn and Sioux Expeditions so he would have been well known to George S. Howard, who served as a scout.

Photograph by Jack Reneau.

Focus on page 29 of map showing railroads of the Connecticut River Valley in 1870. Map shows the railroad line on which George S. Howard worked when his accident occurred in 1870.

Shaw, Robert B. *Down Brakes*. P. R. Macmillan Ltd., London and Geneva. 1961.

A complete history of railroad accidents, safety precautions, and operating practices in the United States from 1831 to 1960. Brief description of severe railroad accident that injured George S. Howard on June 16, 1870, at Athol, Mass. Appendix lists the most serious train accidents since 1831. George's train accident was listed as one of the most severe of the 19th century. Original book found in the AAR library, Wash., D.C.

————. "Serious Railroad Accident," *Providence Daily Journal*, Providence, R.I., Friday morning edition, June 17, 1870, Front Page.

One of first articles detailing serious train accident involving George S. Howard on June 16, 1870.

————. "Shocking Accident on the Vermont and Massachusetts Railroad!" *Boston Morning Journal*, Boston, Mass., Friday morning edition, June 17, 1870, Front Page.

First known newspaper account of train accident on June 16, 1870, involving George S. Howard where three were killed and twenty injured. George had a fractured skull. This seems to be the article other newspapers reproduced as word spread of the wreck. The complete article reproduced in Chapter One of this book.

————. "Shocking Railroad Accident!" *New York Times*, New York, N.Y., Friday afternoon edition, June 17, 1870, Front Page.

Article from morning editions of Boston newspapers is reproduced in the New York Times *that details the train accident at Athol, Mass., on June 16, 1870, involving George S. Howard. In this article, George listed as fatally injured.*

————. "Shooting Affair," *Fitchburg Sentinel*, Fitchburg, Mass., January 19, 1887, page 3.

Updated health report of George S. Howard's condition after shooting January 18. Outlook hopeless for George.

Sollid, Roberta Beed. *Calamity Jane: A Study in Historical Criticism*. The Western Press, Historical Society of Montana, Helena, Mont. 1958.

Historical sketch of one of the great Western female characters who rode as a teamster and guide with the Big Horn Expedition of 1876.

Strahorn, Robert A. "The Big Horn Expedition: An Indian Encampment Destroyed," *Rocky Mountain Tribune (Rocky Mountain News)*, Denver, Colo., April 4, 1876, Front Page.

Detailed account of forced march from Fort Fetterman to Powder River, Battle of Powder River, aftermath of battle, minute-by-minute accounting of battle movements by cavalry, and weather conditions of march. Based upon this account, George's poems about the Battle of Powder River made sense. George's poetry provided much detail that was substantiated by this newspaper account of the campaign. Strahorn filed his report at Old Fort Reno on March 21, 1876, after marching with the troops for fourteen days and covering more than 400 miles in severe winter snow storms. Jerome A. Greene records in his book that Strahorn had this article published in the April 7, 1876, edition, but my copy from the Library of Congress said April 4, and "Tribune." My microfilmed copy is in poor condition. The content of article is the same.

Terrell, John Upton. *Sioux Trail*. McGraw-Hill Book Company, New York, N.Y. 1974.

Explores culture and reactions of Sioux Nation to white settlers, soldiers, and miners into Indian territory during the mid- to late-1800s. Especially helpful was the description of early Sioux history and the tribes of the Sioux Nation. Focus placed on chapter titled, "The Sioux of the Midwestern Prairies and the Middle Great Plains."

————. "Terrible Railroad Accident!" *Providence Evening Press*, Providence, R.I., Friday evening edition, June 17, 1870, Front Page.

Detailed report on serious train accident at Athol, Mass., June 16 involving George S. Howard.

————. "Terrible Railroad Disaster: Frightful Accident on the Vermont and Massachusetts Railroad," *Boston Post*, Boston, Mass., June 17, 1870, Front Page.

One of first detailed articles about serious train accident June 16, involving George S. Howard in which George's skull was crushed.

Terry, Alfred H. *The Field Diary of General Alfred H. Terry: The Yellowstone Expedition, 1876*. Old Army Press, Bellevue, Neb. 1969.

Gen. Terry's field notes of the Yellowstone Expedition, which included activities related to George S. Howard.

Travel Montana Department of Commerce. *Montana*. Montana Department of Commerce, Helena, Mont. 1990.

The 1990 Montana vacation guide book and travel planner book provides colorful highlights of the state's history and important sites discussed in George S. Howard's diary. Of special help are the maps showing the locations of important battle sites and gold rush activities.

U.S. Park Service. *Fort Laramie Historic Buildings Guide*. U.S. Government Printing Office, Wash., D.C. 1987.

This small booklet describes the restored buildings of Fort Laramie National Historic Site, Wyo.

U.S. Park Service. *Little Bighorn Battlefield National Monument* U.S. Government Printing Office, Wash., D.C. 1991.

This pamphlet describes the battlefield and the national monument site for visitors to this famous Western landmark in Montana.

Utley, Robert M. *Frontier Regulars: The U.S. Army and the Indian, 1866–1891.* Macmillan Publishing Co., Inc., New York, N.Y. 1973.

Chapters of special interest were on Fort Phil Kearny (7), Sitting Bull, 1870–76 (14), conquest of the Sioux, 1876–81 (15), Grant's peace policy, 1869–74 (12), the Red River War, 1874–75 (13), and the Battle of Powder River (pages 249 to 251).

Vaughn, J. W. *With Crook at the Rosebud.* University of Nebraska Press, Lincoln and London. 1956.

Details of the Battle of the Rosebud contained in this excellent reference book. The listing of the troops in the battle, by name and rank, were of special interest. The camp at Fort Fetterman, the march along Goose Creek, and the battle itself provide the reader with minute details regarding this event which George S. Howard lived and described in his diary.

Weems, John E. *Death Song: The Last of the Indian Wars.* Doubleday and Company, New York, N.Y. 1976.

One hundred years after the most active year of fighting in 1876, the author provides historical insight into the events of the Indian Wars. Of special interest was Chapter 19 on Col. Custer and the 7th Cavalry, and general orders by Gen. Sheridan on February 7, 1876.

Werner, Fred H. *Before the Little Big Horn.* Werner Publications, Billings, Montana. 1980.

Details the events leading up to the famous "Custer's Last Stand" at the Battle of Little Big Horn. Provides historical perspective for George S. Howard's comments in his diary.

Werner, Fred H. *The Slim Buttes Battle.* Werner Publications, Greeley, Colorado. 1981.

Offers insight and detail of the Battle of Slim Buttes in which George S. Howard fought. Of special interest are the reproduction of official military reports filed by commanding officers which are located in their original form in the National Archives.

Werner, Fred H. *The Soldiers are Coming! The Story of the Reynolds Battle March 17, 1876.*
Werner Publications, Greeley, Colorado. 1982.

*Excellent reference book for the details of the Battle of Powder River and the events before,
during, and after the skirmish. Of special interest is the appendix, which reproduces the
official reports filed by Gen. Crook, Col. Joseph J. Reynolds, Capt. Anson Mills, and Capt.
Henry E. Noyes. The original reports are in the personnel files of these officers at the
National Archives.*

Wyoming Pioneer Association. *Take a Step Back in Time.* Wyoming Travel Commission,
Douglas, Wyo. 1990.

*Brochure describes content of one of the most extensive collections of Western pioneer life
from 1880 to the early 1900s. Many of the artifacts in the museum did not exist for
George S. Howard. The museum is located in Douglas, Wyoming.*

This side view of Spotted Tail (Tshin-tah-las-Kah) was taken in 1872 by Alexander Gardner. George S. Howard would have seen Spotted Tail many times during his five-year enlistment from 1872 to 1877.

Index

ABOUT THE AUTHOR

Susan C. Reneau is the co-author of the Western book, *Colorado's Biggest Bucks and Bulls*, that was released by Colorado Big Game Trophy Records, Inc., of Colorado Springs, in 1983, 1984, 1988, and 1990. She is the co-editor of the book, *Records of North American Big Game, 10th edition*, that was released by the Boone and Crockett Club in 1993.

Susan has written thousands of articles for newspapers and magazines in California, Colorado, Virginia, and Washington, D.C. since 1979. She has coordinated the production and marketing of 36 books since 1984. Susan holds a B.A. in education and communications from the University of Northern Colorado, Greeley, Colorado, and a M.S. in public relations and marketing from American University, Washington, D.C. She is currently writing the second edition to her first book, *Colorado's Biggest Bucks and Bulls, Part II*.

She is the child of a retired Marine Corps officer, so she was raised in California, Colorado, Chicago, Hawaii, North Carolina, South Carolina, and Virginia. As an adult, Susan has lived in California, Colorado, Kentucky, Montana, and Virginia, with her husband and three sons. They have been married since April 6, 1974.

Acknowledgements

Book design and layout:
                    Jack Reneau

Copy editor:
            Carol J. Kersavage
            Outdoor Writers Association of America, Inc.
            State College, Pennsylvania

Cover design:
            Meerkat Graphics Centre
            Lolo, Montana

Illustrator:
            Lori A. Scoffield
            Pocatello, Idaho

Printing and binding:
                    Publishers Press
                    Salt Lake City, Utah

Typesetting:
            Colorado Typographics
            Loveland, Colorado